NEW TEACHERS HELPING NEW TEACHERS:
PRESERVICE PEER COACHING

by
Elizabeth A. McAllister
and
Gloria A. Neubert

ERIC

Clearinghouse on Reading,
English, and Communication

EDINFO
PRESS

Published by ERIC Clearinghouse on Reading, English, and Communication and EDINFO Press, Indiana University, P.O. Box 5953, Bloomington, IN 47407

Editor: Warren Lewis
Production: Lauren Bongiani Gottlieb
Cover design and photography: David J. Smith

ERIC (an acronym for Educational Resources Information Center) is a national network of 16 clearinghouses, each of which is responsible for building the ERIC database by identifying and abstracting various educational resources, including research reports, curriculum guides, conference papers, journal articles, and government reports. The Clearinghouse on Reading, English, and Communication (ERIC/REC) collects educational information specifically related to reading, English, journalism, speech, and theater at all levels. ERIC/REC also covers interdisciplinary areas, such as media studies, reading and writing technology, mass communication, language arts, critical thinking, literature, and many aspects of literacy.

This publication was prepared with partial funding from the U.S. Department of Education, under contract no. RR93002011. Contractors undertaking such projects under government sponsorship are encouraged to express freely their judgment in professional and technical matters. Points of view or opinions, however, do not necessarily represent the official view or opinions of the U.S. Department of Education.

Library of Congress Cataloging-in-Publication Data

McAllister, Elizabeth A.

New teachers helping new teachers : preservice peer coaching / by Elizabeth A. McAllister and Gloria A. Neubert.

P.   cm.

Includes bibliographical references (p.   ).

ISBN 1-883790-14-X

1. Teachers—Training of—Maryland—Longitudinal studies. 2. Student teaching—Maryland—Longitudinal studies. 3. Follow-up in teacher training—Maryland—Longitudinal studies. 4. Mentors in education—Maryland— Longitudinal studies. 5. Towson State University.   I. Neubert, Gloria A.   II. ERIC Clearinghouse on Reading, English, and Communication.   III. Title.

LB2167.M3M32   1995

370'.71'09752—dc20

94-49407
CIP

TABLE OF CONTENTS

(Table of Contents, continued)

ADVISORY BOARD

A WORD TO NEW TEACHERS AND EXPERIENCED TEACHERS ALIKE

Research in teacher preparation is not static; it continues to grow in breadth and depth. Educators of preservice teachers are eager to be as effective in purveying theoretical knowledge as they are in assisting their novices to carry the knowledge into practical application in the classroom. New teachers are at least as eager as their teacher-educators are to learn the newest and best ways to teach.

With this concern for theory and practice in mind, we undertook a two-and-one-half year-long research study with 135 preservice teachers at Towson State University (Maryland). Our results include an explanation of change in the field-experience portion of a teacher education program to include preservice peer coaching. We recount scenarios of student experiences in which peer coaching was used, description of the students, the training to coach one another, results of this endeavor, and ways that teacher educators can use this information in their teaching of teachers. Seasoned teacher educators will use this text to teach new teachers. Preservice teachers will follow these guidelines as a part of their training in preservice peer coaching. The *New Teachers' Peer Coaching Workbook* at the end (pp. 107–114) is for teacher-educators and preservice teacher-students alike. Use the *New Teachers' Peer Coaching Workbook* as an easy way to implement what we learned as a result of our research and application.

These chapters were written in "heteroglossic" form (McCarthy and Fishman, 1991) in that the text reflects both the individual and collective perspectives of the authors. Thus, chapters 2 and 3 were written from the perspective of the course instructor, Elizabeth McAllister; chapter 4 was written from the perspective of the trainer, Gloria Neubert; chapters 1 and 5 were written from the perspectives of both. We use the pronoun "we" throughout for the comfort of the reader.

We hope that you will catch the excitement of this experience that we shared, glean new insights into preservice teacher development, and use this information to embark upon a new, rewarding experience in teaching and learning about new teachers helping new teachers to become good teachers.

Elizabeth A. McAllister

Gloria A. Neubert

CHAPTER 1

FACILITATING REFLECTIVE THINKING IN PRESERVICE TEACHER EDUCATION

Preservice teacher-education students usually enter field experiences armed with knowledge of a variety of teaching strategies. For example, most have heard lectures and have read about, discussed, and analyzed various models of instruction, classroom management strategies, curriculum organization patterns, questioning strategies, strategies for special-needs students, etc. They usually can explain the theory and research support for these strategies, and they have even had opportunities to practice some of the strategies in the protected environment of the campus through simulated or clinical experiences.

Each of these experiences moves preservice teachers along to the point of actual engagement with students in the real world of school classrooms by actively engaging them in the analysis of the strategies presented during their campus coursework. Teacher educators, motivated in recent years by their belief in a theory of learning that views learning as a constructive process, have shaped their courses and programs so that preservice students are cognitively engaged in learning experiences as opposed to merely listening to professors' lectures and passively absorbing the information presented. Teaching is viewed not as the transmission of knowledge, and learning is not only listening, memorization, and indoctrination, but cognitive engagement during which the professor and the students share mutually their backgrounds of experiences, theoretical constructs, and plans for innovation. This style of teaching seems especially appropriate in a course in which a teacher is teaching other teachers how to teach. Thus, they all collaborate cognitively in the discussion of teaching strategies; build their knowledge base through reading, observing, listening and discussing; and then evaluate, explore, and apply the strategies to be learned.

For example, a teacher educator who chooses to present the strategy of "reader response" to preservice teacher-education students may begin by having the students recall through writing a memory—good or bad—of their experiences learning about poetry in elementary or secondary school. Professor and students share their experiences, with the professor leading the discussion so that everyone may articulate their memories of rights and wrongs suffered during the interpretation of poetry in school. The professor then teaches students to interpret a poem using the reader response approach. After this direct experience with the approach, the students operationally define the method on the basis of their experiences during the demonstration lesson. The professor then has the students view a videotape of a sixth-grade teacher using reader response with his students. Next, the professor and preservice teachers engage in a critical analysis of the lesson, which eventuates in a discussion of the advantages and limitations of, and alternatives to, this literary approach. "Why," "when," and "if" questions are coupled with "how" questions. Finally, each student writes a lesson plan, uses the reader response approach to literature in a simulated teaching situation, and cooperatively critiques the lesson with peers and the professor. In this way, the preservice teachers are actively learning about the reader response approach; they are not just passively receiving the information from their professor. They are doing, not just hearing about. Thus the learners construct their own knowledge, as opposed to relying passively on the teacher-educator or someone else to "cover the curriculum" for them. The result is that students learn more through active learning than they do through passive instruction.

This kind of active learning facilitates preservice teachers' understanding of the what, how, and why of teaching strategies; it prepares them for the next essential step in their preparation as teachers—field experiences during which they apply these strategies in an actual classroom setting beset with all the distracting variables of the real school room full of real students.

Unfortunately, the cognitive engagement experienced on campus in courses does not always maintain itself during field experiences. Consider the typical field experience of the preservice teacher: One student-teacher is placed with one supervising classroom teacher for a short duration, typically one day per week for one semester. The student eventually plans and teaches a few lessons, and is evaluated through feedback from the classroom teacher. This feedback usually comes in the form of written and/or oral comments presented in expository form from the very busy classroom teacher distracted by routine demands. That is, the supervising classroom teacher tells the student-teacher what was good about the lesson, what should be changed, and how it should be changed. Time is short, and an opportunity for the preservice teacher to engage in self-analytic reflection, prompted by questioning from the classroom teacher, as was the case in on-campus courses, may not arise, and even if it does, it will likely be a less thorough discussion. Besides, many supervising teachers do not encourage preservice teachers to examine their teaching, to question current practices, or to consider alternative approaches, because reflective thinking may be foreign to their own practice and dispositions, and they may view reflection as a threat to their normal way of operating.

Thus, during the first, crucial experiences in the real world of the classroom, preservice teachers typically become the passive recipients of someone else's information with little or no opportunity to engage in active dialogue and reflection. In short, the usual field experience is not the educative equivalent of most good classes taught in our departments and schools of education. Peer coaching as reflection, we suggest, is a way to improve this situation.

REFLECTION

Reflection, or reflective thinking, is a type of critical thinking, a form of suspended judgement. It is thinking that engages practitioners in examining and raising questions about a lesson taught or an administrative practice. It is time allocated to asking, "What is *really* going on in this classroom?" When educators reflect, they are ultimately employing active cognitive engagement; they are not just executing and/or observing educational events, but are analyzing the events. They ask questions, such as:

> *"Did this approach result in learning . . . ?"*
>
> *"Why was this strategy so effective/ineffective today?" "Would my students have been more cooperative if I . . . ?" "What would happen if the school . . . ?"*
>
> *"How will students be affected if . . . ?"*

"Why am I teaching this . . . ?"

"Is there a better way to . . . ?"

By asking such questions, educators are not merely other-reliant for their growth because they actively pursue the analysis of their own lessons or circumstances. They assume the power to determine the directions of their classrooms and schools.

Roth (1989, p. 32) has summarized the processes one engages in during reflection:

1. Question what, why, and how one does things; ask what, why, and how others do things.

2. Emphasize inquiry as a tool of learning.

3. Suspend judgment, wait for sufficient data, or self-validate.

4. Seek alternatives.

5. Keep an open mind.

6. Compare and contrast.

7. Seek the framework, theoretical basis, underlying rationale (of behaviors, methods, techniques, programs).

8. View from various perspectives.

9. Identify and test assumptions (their own and those of others); seek conflicting evidence.

10. Put into different/varied contexts.

11. Ask "what if . . .?"

12. Ask for others' ideas and viewpoints.

13. Adapt and adjust to instability and change.

14. Function within uncertainty, complexity, and variety.

15. Hypothesize.

16. Consider consequences.

17. Validate what is given or believed.

18. Synthesize and test.

19. Seek, identify, and resolve problems ("problem setting," "problem solving").

20. Initiate after thinking through (alternatives, consequences) or putting into context.

21. Analyze—what makes it work? In what context would it not work?

22. Evaluate—what worked, what didn't, and why?

23. Use prescriptive models (behavioral models, protocols) only when adapted to the situation.

24. Make decisions in practice of the profession (knowledge created in use).

Van Manen (1977), a social scientist, organized reflective thinking into three levels. These levels were then applied to teaching by Zeichner and Liston. Level one is "technical rationality," a concern with efficient and effective application of pedagogical and curricular knowledge to attain given educational aims. (Zeichner and Liston, 1987) Level two is "practical action," in which the teacher is concerned about "the underlying assumptions and consequences of pedagogical action." (Liston and Zeichner, 1987, p.2) Level three, "critical reflection," is attention to "the moral implications of pedagogical actions and the structure of schooling." (Liston and Zeichner, 1987, pp. 2-3)

Experience has shown that, left on their own, novice educators do not *automatically* take on a reflective stance. For most preservice students, if a lesson is completed without a calamity, it is usually considered a success, no more thought is given to it, and attention is moved to the preparation and/or teaching of the next lesson. Time allocated for reflection is not a natural part of the student's teaching cycle. For students not trained in reflective thinking, the following is a typical analysis and evaluation of a lesson:

> *Everyone seemed to catch on quickly to the concepts. The whole class aced the puzzle.*

Yet research has shown that reflection can be fostered (Ferguson, 1989) and may, indeed, be developmental, that is, engaging in lower level reflection may be a prerequisite for moving on to higher levels. (Ross, 1989)

Several conditions appear to foster reflection. First, preservice teachers must have opportunities for reflection. They must experience the real world of the schools through field experiences, and they must have models of reality through campus simulations and clinical experiences (e.g., focused video-tapes, actual lesson demonstrations and/or case studies), all with sufficient time allocated for analysis and reflection. Only through such opportunities will novices develop the background of experience (schemata) needed for growth in reflection.

Second, an appropriately reflective opportunity is one that actively engages the preservice teacher. A teacher-educator or a supervising teacher who begins a conference after observing a class taught by a student teacher with a statement such as the following is not likely to encourage active engagement of the preservice teacher:

You did several things right in that lesson. I'll go over these with you, and I'm also going to suggest three things you can do differently.

Instead, the debriefing conference becomes a passive experience, with the student being lectured to by a teacher-educator and/or a classroom super-vising teacher. This is not the same thing as, nor does it take the place of, active, engaged, experiential reflection. Under passive conditions, the wrong people are getting practice in reflective thinking. Expository presentations are opportunities for the experts to reflect on the lesson, but the preservice teach-ers will derive relatively little benefit from listening to one more lecture.

Third, inherent in reflection is an audience, a sounding board for one's ideas, an interlocutor, a person with whom to dialogue. Programs that set up reflective opportunities " . . . as a form of *individual* problem solving, that lack a concept of community, send an unfortunate message to the neophyte about the role and responsibilities of educators within a democratic society." (Bullough, 1989, p. 19) Talking (aloud or on paper) to another person helps us to explore, monitor, and evaluate our thoughts. We often talk to discover what we know, what we do not know, what we want to know, and what we believe or do not believe. The audience serves to validate, extend, modify, support, or reject what we think through by interacting with us and by pro-viding feedback that can happen only in this collaborative process. The con-cept of dialogue is essential to the constructivist theory of active learning espoused here. Dialogue provides the avenue for reciprocal learning when the dialogue takes place between preservice teachers.

Finally, reflective opportunities should be "guided." Preservice students cannot be expected to be successful at reflection merely by being told: "Reflect!" That is like ordering a fat person: "Be thin!" Just as teacher-educators guide reflection on campus through modeling and eliciting questions when models of reality are analyzed, they must provide scaffolding in the form of guided practice in reflection for preservice teachers before and during field opportunities.

PEER COACHING AS REFLECTION

We believe that reflection is necessary for maximizing professional growth; therefore, it is not a question of "Should reflection be a part of pre-service programs?" but rather "How can reflection be incorporated into pre-service programs?"

We believe that the requirement to reflect ought not to reside solely in field experiences, and should certainly not be delayed until the student-teaching or full-time internship phase, which is usually scheduled at the end of the preservice program. A late introduction of reflection can result in resistance because the reflective stance is usually foreign to preservice-teachers' repertoires. (Zeichner and Liston, 1987) Preservice teachers need to acquire the disposition of reflective practitioners early in their professional careers; therefore, on-campus program components often include requirements encouraging guided reflection. Reflection is promoted when preservice teachers write learning logs or journals, analyze prepared case studies and/or videotape protocols, critique peers' lesson plans, microteach and critique the lessons, and participate in reflective seminars concurrent with field experiences. Some of these same techniques—learning logs or journals, student-written case studies, videotaping of lessons taught—can also be used during field work to continue fostering reflective thinking.

Through our work with preservice teachers, we have learned that one of the most successful staff development techniques originally used with inservice teachers, *PEER COACHING*, can catapult preservice teachers from a non-reflective to a reflective stance during their early field experiences.

COACHING, a concept originally described by Joyce and Showers (1980), is the in-class assistance provided by an outside trainer or facilitator or by an in-school colleague for a teacher who is attempting to incorporate a new teaching skill, strategy, or approach that is foreign to his/her teaching repertoire. The term, *peer coaching*, is used when the "in-class assistance" that a teacher receives is provided by a colleague—often another teacher in the school—as opposed to the assistance of an expert or facilitator from outside the school. This colleague 1) assists the teacher in planning the lesson, focusing on the new skill; 2) observes the teacher executing the lesson, paying specific attention to the application of the desired skill and usually making focused, written notes; and 3) debriefs with the teacher at the conclusion of the lesson concerning the application of the new skill.

The literature on peer coaching with inservice teachers is almost unanimous in the conclusion that coaching, appropriately used, is a highly successful method for helping teachers apply new skills. (See Brandt, 1989; Neubert, 1988; Strother, 1989.) Coached teachers use new approaches more skillfully, more appropriately, more frequently, and with greater long-term retention than do trained, but uncoached teachers. (Baker and Showers, 1984)

Inservice teachers' anecdotal reports evidence their enthusiasm for peer coaching. Teachers, who are sometimes reluctant to seek help from supervisors and administrators, seem to embrace peer coaching because it is not associated with individuals of higher rank who *evaluate* them. The peer coaching arrangement provides personal facilitation—moral support—to the teacher who finds him/herself in the precarious position of a learner.

Teaching is typically a solitary act. During peer coaching, peers provide affirmation that can reduce the disequilibrium and loneliness associated with trying to apply a new skill. This positive attitude is particularly evident when the inservice teachers' coaching situation is set up as reciprocal coaching, as opposed to one-way coaching. In reciprocal coaching, a pair of teachers alternate roles—coaching, and being coached by, each other.

For example, two teachers might want to apply what they learned about cooperative learning from reading a journal article, or Teacher A may wish to learn to use cooperative learning, while Teacher B chooses to focus on a writing process technique new to her. In either case, reciprocal coaching would involve both Teacher A and Teacher B in conferencing and exchanging visits to the other's classroom to serve as coach, and both teachers would be in the role of the teacher who is the learner. In contrast, with one-way coaching, two teachers are involved, but only one teacher is attempting to apply a new skill, strategy, or approach; therefore, the role of coach is assumed by only one teacher. Reciprocal peer coaching appears to be the more favored form, for both teachers experience the disequilibrium of the learner, as well as the professional pride that results from serving as coach.

Another affective benefit of peer coaching is the new sense of professionalism provided the teachers. This is peers inquiring about teaching with other peers. It is empowerment of teachers to be change agents with and for their colleagues.

Finally, research has reported the effectiveness of coaching in promoting reflection on the part of inservice teachers. (Pasch, et al. 1990) This is not surpising, considering that *appropriately* executed coaching involves teachers in thinking critically about the application of new skills/strategies/approaches. They are analyzing their own lessons and those of their coaching partner; they are asking "Why?" and "What if?" That is, when one is coaching or being coached, one is engaged in the thinking processes required of the reflective practitioner.

The benefits that inservice teachers enjoy from peer coaching were the motivators for building peer coaching into our own preservice teacher-education program. If it works for inservice teachers, we reasoned, could it not also work for preservice-teachers? Would peer coaching help preservice teachers apply skills, strategies, and approaches? Would it encourage reflection? Would the new teachers value peer coaching?

What follows is an example of peer coaching between two preservice teachers enrolled in a one-semester, junior-level curriculum course which included a one-day-per-week field experience. This coaching episode took place early in the semester. Daphne and Staci were coaching partners. Staci, in the capacity of coach, had observed Daphne's lesson the previous day, and this is the transcript of their debriefing conference.

STACI AND DAPHNE:
PEER COACHING CONFERENCE DIALOGUE

STACI (coach): I thought your lesson was very good!

DAPHNE (teacher): Thank you!

STACI: The positive reinforcement you used throughout the lesson was good. It encouraged the students to participate in the discussion.

DAPHNE: I always try to praise the kids whenever I can.

STACI: I also thought that discussing the vocabulary words before reading the story helped the students understand the reading material better.

DAPHNE: My skill focus was reading comprehension, so I'm glad you noticed that.

STACI: Yes, it was apparent from the discussion of the story that the students comprehended the material. Also, having them draw pictures of what they would like if they were a clown was an excellent follow-up activity. It really allowed the kids to use their creativity and imagination.

DAPHNE: Thanks. I really think they enjoyed drawing the pictures. Their art work will look great up on the wall.

STACI: Yes, it will. I thought the guided reading method you used was good, but what other methods of guided reading could you have used?

DAPHNE: Well, they could have read the whole story silently to themselves. I could have read the whole story to them. Or, I could have instructed them to read a paragraph or page silently, asked them questions on that paragraph or page, and continued that way.

STACI: Why do you think this story was included in this curriculum?

DAPHNE: Because kids need a variety of sources of information about the world around them. Some children might not have the opportunity to experience things such as a circus; therefore, by supplying them with stories such as "From Jesters to Joeys," and activities to enhance comprehension, kids can learn about the world in which they live.

STACI: I loved the circus when I was a kid. Actually, I still do.

DAPHNE: So do I!

STACI: I noticed that while a child was reading part of the story, some of the other students weren't following along with the text. Do you think the children would follow the story more closely if they read silently rather than out loud?

DAPHNE: I would be willing to try that because having each child read a paragraph out loud didn't work for everyone.

STACI: Do you think having the kids write down the answers to the focus questions would improve comprehension?

DAPHNE: I think the students would tend to write down other students' answers instead of thinking for themselves as they do in group discussion.

STACI: You're right. I didn't think of that. Again, I really enjoyed watching your lesson.

DAPHNE: Thanks! I get to watch yours next week.

STACI: Oh, yes. I have one more question to ask you. Why did you decide to bring in library books to show the students?

DAPHNE: I thought they would be a good motivation. Also, they had the chance to read them later in the day.

STACI: That was a great idea. Maybe I can do something like that for my lesson.

Following this coaching session, both students reflected in writing on their experience.

REFLECTIVE COMMENTS OF THE COACH (STACI)

I thought Daphne interacted very well with the students. She seemed very comfortable with them, as they were with her. She used a lot of positive reinforcement, which I think is very important. She knew the material she was teaching, which showed advance planning and preparation. Our styles of teaching are very similar; therefore, I think we work well together.

The main thing I learned from observing Daphne and conferring with her afterwards is to be flexible in my teaching methods. If one method doesn't work with the whole group, try another method, or adapt my teaching strategies for one or more individuals. When I suggested to Daphne that a different approach to guided reading should be used because some of the children weren't following along, she was very open to the alternative. Being flexible also helps when one comes across an unusual situation.

Daphne brought up a point that really stuck in my mind. She said that some children may not have the opportunity to experience things other children do, such as a circus. Well, I thought that everybody had been to a circus! Then I realized that there was a lot of truth in what she said. When I am teaching, I may have students that come from disadvantaged families. I must make an effort to be sensitive to these students and not make assumptions about their background like I did while conversing with Daphne.

REFLECTIVE DECISIONS OF THE TEACHER (DAPHNE)

The main problem that I found in trying to teach my lesson was keeping the students' attention focused on the story during the group reading. My coach suggested that instead of having the students read the story orally, I should have them read one paragraph at a time silently, and then ask specific questions after they read one page. I agreed and have since tried that method. It works very well in keeping the attention of the students, as well as in aiding their comprehension of the story. I had previously waited until the reading of the story was complete before asking the recall questions. Frequently, the students had a difficult time remembering because they had to read the entire story before answering the questions. Therefore, by reading the story a piece at a time and answering the questions as they read, the students gained a better understanding of the story and appeared to feel more positive about the answers they gave.

We observe that reflective thinking is emerging in these novice teachers even at this early stage in their teacher preparation. Already many of the reflective processes delineated by Roth are being used. (See above for Roth's list. Numbers below refer to specific processes identified by Roth.) For example, students are evaluating "what worked, what didn't, and why" (#22). Each is questioning how (#1) comprehension was and could be facilitated better through alternative (#4) reading and questioning procedures. The coach, Staci, asks "what if?" questions (#11); for example, "Do you think the children would follow the story more closely if they read silently rather than out loud?" In her written "Relective Comments," Staci articulates her belief in the importance of being "flexible," or as Roth labels it, "Keep an open mind" (#5). Daphne "initiate[s] after thinking through . . . alternatives" (#20), that is, she reports in her written "Reflective Comments" trying the silent reading with interspersed-questions approach, then proceeds to contrast (#6) these consequences to the way she had initially taught the reading.

This transcript and these two reflections reveal that these two preservice teachers are reflecting primarily on the level of "technical rationality" because they are focusing on the effective application of pedagogical and curricular knowledge concerning oral versus silent reading and question placement for reading comprehension. (See discussion of Zeichner and Liston's reflective levels above.) Staci evidences some inclination toward level two, "practical action," when she reports in her written "Reflective Coments" her recognition that she should not assume, but should be responsible for developing, students' adequate backgrounds of experience. She has identified a personal assumption and is questioning its educational consequences for her students.

SUMMARY

The dialogue and reflective writings of Staci and Daphne are typical of our students' work. They are evidence of the reflective thought of novices when the four conditions for fostering reflection become a required part of a preservice course. First, students are provided opportunities to engage in reflection during their early field experiences. Second, students themselves are actively engaged in debriefing the lesson by engaging in coaching, as opposed to their passively listening to someone else analyze their teaching. Third, each student has a person with whom to dialogue, a peer with whom to analyze, explore, and share. Students are not working in isolation, limited by their own ideas. Fourth, preservice peer coaching is "guided." It is structured so that students almost cannot help but be reflective. The students must plan, observe each other's lessons, conference using a specified format that prompts reflection, and write follow-up reflective summaries.

Preservice peer coaching has become a valued component of the course for us and for our students. Our preservice teachers show evidence of reflecting, of applying skills that they learn about in methodology courses, and of having a positive attitude towards peer coaching. Staci's end-of-semester evaluation of this project echoes the collective opinion of our students:

My coaching partner helped me feel very good about myself as I tried new teaching strategies! She praised my teaching, and pointed out, as well as helped me remember, different ways I could have taught the lesson. I later incorporated these ideas on my own and they worked well.

CHAPTER 2

RETHINKING THE MAKING
OF TEACHERS

THE OLD WAY

The component of field experiences in teacher education at Towson State University—like many other schools of education—is distributed across three semesters, starting with the junior year. Semester one is Field Studies. During this course, students are placed with an experienced teacher in a pub-lic- school setting for one-half day each week. They observe and act as teacher aides, working with a few students at a time. Time is also spent familiarizing themselves with teachers' responsibilities, school schedules, and other teach-ers that serve the schools.

The second field experience semester is the one during which students are placed in the public school one full day each week. They move from being an observer and aide to actually teaching all subjects to the total class by the end of the semester. Early in this experience students take on the preparation and teaching of one or two subjects, and they add another each week until they are teaching a continuous three days with the supervising teacher out of the room, but close at hand. This build-up of student contact and teaching responsibilities is designed to prepare the students for the final field experi-ence, solo student teaching.

Though each student works with a supervising teacher and gradually takes on more teaching responsibilities, the experiences tend to be void of in-depth analysis of self-growth or a grasp of the art of teaching. Assignments and preparations march on mechanically and deliberately. Student teachers have no one to bounce ideas off of—no really close colleague to be in on things that happened, or failed to happen, in the classroom context. Questions and concerns typically remain superficial; problems are ignored or endured alone.

This field experience was part of a course, "The Curriculum and the Elementary Child" that included a class period on campus for debriefing, where we tried to encourage the students to talk about their experiences in the school settings. No amount of probing and cajoling could bring out the insights that we thought were budding inside the minds of those young teachers. Their responses were rather concrete, but essentially uninformative. The students felt that their lessons had gone well, in those cases when they were able to finish with no obvious catastrophe. When describing lessons, they would often pull out the written plans and read them aloud. It was as though the execution of the lesson had been done by someone else. Doubtless, there was no further thought about it. Their attitude was "no looking back; on to the next lesson!"

Student teachers' reticence to delve too deeply is understandable. They have to find some way to apply a wealth of "new" ideas and content in the classroom setting. They are overwhelmed. They are unsure of themselves. It seemed to us that the students thought it unimportant to ask WHY a lesson had gone well or poorly.

This pivotal semester in preservice teacher training is important enough to find some way to help the students realize that they can reflect on their decisions about teaching; and that they can grow as effective teachers. They lack self-confidence, and this problem is met head-on by providing them with training to coach one another, thus having a colleague to share in insights and growth.

To provide a bridge from the university classroom and new theories to which they are being introduced, we designed an experience in peer coaching. A discussion of this new way follows.

THE NEW WAY

Dissatisfaction leads to change! Frustration leads to extreme divergence from the norm of mediocre sameness!

Concerns about student teachers failing to become reflective teachers led us to explore the avenue of peer coaching as a "new" way to approach self-assessment of student teaching experiences. Peer coaching had been proven to be an effective vehicle for teachers already in the field to improve their teaching techniques (Neubert, 1988). Surely it would work for preservice student-teachers as well. With this determination in mind, we embarked on the brand-new approach to the intermediate field-experience semester.

Preservice Peer Coaching Theory

Observing a practicing teacher who is experienced is quite different from observing a peer. The expectations change. A student teacher has higher expectations of the practicing teacher than that of a peer who has the same level of training and experience.

Observing a peer generates comradery during the teaching experience. The comfort level is higher because peers can relate to each other about common problems. The partners understand one another and share the same informality of communication and interaction. This, therefore, becomes an opportunity to learn from one another and from themselves without someone looking over their shoulders.

Expectations of Preservice Peer Coaching

As professors of preservice teachers who have had little experience in the field, we think that peer coaching is the answer to meeting their immediate needs. It will provide them with an outlet for expression and exploration. It will offer a safety-net to catch failures and gain new insights. It will give them an avenue by which they can observe each other and reflect on self, during the act of teaching.

Getting Started

Realizing that preservice teachers need structure and a sense of direction, we implemented training in peer coaching. All they knew about this semester was that they would be very busy. They knew that they would experience being REAL teachers for the first time, this just prior to senior student teaching.

During the first class period of the semester, we laid out the entire semester course requirements. When the peer coaching project was described, we all but had a mutiny on our hands. The students had so little self-confidence that the peer coaching project seemed to be more than they could handle. At the end of the class period, one student said, "I think I'll DIE this semester." We told her, and the rest of the class, to hang in there with us and promised: " Everyone WILL walk out vertical!" Not only did they walk out vertically, but also they walked out confident and raring to student-teach. They became insightful, reflective young teachers who knew what they were doing, and WHY it worked. What more can an educator give to preservice teachers at this stage in their professional training?

Peer Coaching Assignment

We paired students who had been placed in public schools, one day a week during the semester, with experienced classroom teachers. Each week, the student teachers also came to the university campus for a two-hour class in Elementary Curriculum. Content included developing lesson plans, learning teaching models and strategies (which would be practiced in the schools), questioning strategies, instructional objectives, classroom management, multicultural issues, school organization, curriculum organizational patterns, and teacher responsibilities. It is a packed course, charged with emotions and expectations.

The peer partners met together to discuss concerns that the preservice teacher—the one who would be teaching—wanted to concentrate upon during the peer coaching conference. The student who observed the lesson was the coach. During the lesson, the coach recorded observations, using a special format involving three verbs: PRAISE, QUESTION, POLISH.(See Chapter 4, Training for Coaching, p. 89). Immediately following the teaching episode, the student teachers met to debrief. At this time, the coach led the conference. Instant dialogue affords the teacher an opportunity to reflect on and to verbalize "what happened" and to ponder what might have made the lesson more effective. Through reflection, the teacher gains insight to improve instruction by anticipating, generating, and adapting delivery.

During this debriefing dialogue, student teachers are reflecting on the planning, delivery, and outcomes of their lessons. Both students are adapting their own schemas about the act of teaching through this experience. Each student will respond to the teaching/coaching experience in the report. The debriefing session is the pivot of the coaching activity.

PEER COACHING REPORT

After each student has taught two lessons and observed and coached two lessons, they write a peer coaching report. In this report, each student writes from the coach's perspective. They include the lesson plans, the coaching forms, and the coaching dialogue during each conference. These reports become the "proof of the pudding" in that they provide concrete evidence of student thought, reflection, and metacognitive growth about the act of teaching while "in the act" of teaching. The student who taught the lesson writes Reflective Decisions following the coaching session. The teacher includes insights gained, changes that would be made if this lesson could be taught again, new awareness learned during the debriefing. The partner who observed the lesson writes Reflective Comments following the conference with the "teacher." The "coach" explores what was learned by observing a partner's lesson.

CHAPTER 3

PEER COACHING SCENARIOS

SCENARIO INTRODUCTION

The partners followed a prescribed schedule for their peer-coaching assignment. Included here are the peer-coaching steps, peer-coaching terms used in their reports, and the scenario organization and coding used by us to interpret the effectiveness of this project.

PEER COACHING STEPS

1. Preservice teacher writes the lesson plan.

2. Planning Conference: Preservice teacher and coach meet to establish observation focus.

3. Lesson Execution/Observation: Preservice teacher teaches the lesson while the coach records observations on the Peer Coaching Form.

4. Debriefing Conference: Preservice teacher and coach engage in a dialogue conference.

5. The preservice teacher writes a Reflective Decisions Statement.

6. The coach writes Reflective Comments.

7. Assessment: The lesson plan, peer coaching dialogue conference, reflective decisions (teacher), and reflective comments (coach) provide documentation for interpretation and assessment of the peer coaching experience.

PEER COACHING TERMS

1. Praise: List of encouraging statements from the coach; what was effective and why

2. Question: List of questions for the coach to use during the dialogue conference

3. Polish: Decisions about lesson changes

4. Conference Dialogue: Transcription of the debriefing conference

SCENARIO ORGANIZATION AND CODING

1. Description of the lesson

2. Conference Dialogue: Statements that show reflection or insight will be italicized.

3. Reflective Comments (coach)

4. Reflective Decisions (teacher)

5. Student Growth in Reflective Insight (interpretation of effectiveness of peer coaching)

6. Peer Coaching Form

7. Lesson Plan

PEER COACHING SCENARIO #1
DEBBIE AND STACEY: BALANCED PARTICIPATION

Debbie and Stacey were partners in the peer-coaching experience. In this episode, Stacey is the teacher and Debbie is acting as coach; observing, recording, and leading the debriefing conference. The lesson that Stacey taught focused on teaching metric measurement to second-graders. See the lesson plan on p. 32, below.

During the preplanning phase, the peers conferred to identify "student participation" as the skill that was Stacey's concern. She asked Debbie to document student participation to determine whether or not all or most of the students were actively engaged while she was teaching.

Debbie designed the Skill Application Form, shown below, to tally student participation and response while instruction was in progress. She also used the Praise-Question-Polish format to record observations during the lesson. This enabled Debbie to lead the debriefing conference after the teaching event was completed.

Statements of reflection and insight about pedagogical principles will be italicized in the reflective summaries.

CONFERENCE DIALOGUE

DEBBIE   Let's first review the Skill Application Form. As you asked each question, I recorded the number of students who volunteered to answer, along with the name of the student you called upon. Of the 22 students in the class, you called on ll different students to answer. Also, I noticed that there were probably another 5 or 6 who had their hands up at various times but were not selected to answer. So, I would say that you were able to maintain the interest of most of the students, at least for the initial phase of the lesson.

STACEY   When I gave each group a bag of beans, telling them to come up and weigh them, do you think that I had too many groups and they became bored?

DEBBIE   After the second group, those waiting at their seats seemed to be getting tired of waiting for their turns to come. They weren't really that interested in watching the other groups. Also, those who finished weighing their beans were no longer paying attention.

STACEY   I myself realized after about the second group that it was getting boring, and, wondered whether or not I should stop or let the others have their turns. But, I knew that if I stopped, the groups would complain, so I let them continue. I agree that it did drag out. What activity do you think that I might use next time?

DEBBIE   Maybe a comparison activity, where you would hold up a bag to be weighed next to those that had already been weighed. Each group could look at the bags and decide which would weigh more, or they could rank the weights. You could record their predictions on the board. That way, the whole class has an interest in the weight of each group's bag. Then they would be watching instead of talking or fooling around.

STACEY   That sounds like a GOOD idea!

DEBBIE   Also, do you think that when each group had to pick the correct number of 1 and 5 gram blocks to balance their bag of beans that it was a bit too abstract for them to understand? What do you think of putting a chart on the board that would list a few common objects along with their weights in grams or kilograms? That way, students could look at their bags of beans and pick the object that they think would weigh about the same. Then they would be comparing one concrete object with another, instead of going directly from the concrete to the abstract.

STACEY   Okay. I think that would work great, and the lesson would move along more smoothly.

DEBBIE   I thought that the way you used a variety of objects along with the balance and the spring scale was a good way to help the students understand an abstract concept like weights. Also, they're probably not so familiar with weight in metric units—grams and kilograms.

STACEY   Do you think the children understood how to use the spring scale as well as they did the balance?

DEBBIE   How did you feel about it? Do you think it may have helped if you had shown the spring scale at the same time that you introduced the balance and worked with comparing the objects that are to be weighed by each instrument? When you passed the beans out and then tried to explain the spring scale, students were more interested in the beans than in that scale.

STACEY   I had planned to introduce the spring scale with the balance, but with everything I was trying to do, I completely forgot until that moment.

DEBBIE   I really liked the way that you had the objects in a pouch and let the students pull each one out. They did not know what was in there, and that made them excited and interested. I also liked the way that, during the lesson, you corrected the students who were misbehaving. You didn't miss a beat as you corrected them—the lesson kept right on flowing along.

STACEY   I'm glad that it didn't disrupt the lesson. I was worried that it would.

DEBBIE   I also noticed that at periodic intervals, you asked if anyone had any questions and if everyone understood what you were explaining. It gave you a chance to take care of misunderstandings immediately. I have a question. When students were picking the objects out of the pouch and you were placing them in the balance, had you weighed them ahead of time so that you knew they would balance?

STACEY   No. I did not plan for them to balance evenly. I was surprised, too.

DEBBIE   The students thought it was really neat that they balanced. Do you think that when you introduced the group activity, it might have been better to wait until after the explanation to pass out the beans? Otherwise, could you have held up the beans for each group as they were coming up to weigh them? Once you gave them their bags of beans, it was all over as far as paying attention to anything you were saying to them. They were looking at the beans and playing catch with the bags. I had visions of hundreds of beans on the floor!

STACEY   So did I! I think that would have made the transition from discussion to activity go a lot smoother.

DEBBIE   I thought the idea to have the small group activity at that point in the lesson was good. It not only provided a hands-on experience but also it pulled everything together. You were so enthusiastic about the lesson! That feeling carried over to the students as they were weighing their beans. They also got excited and tried to predict the number of blocks needed to balance the beans. All in all, I thought your lesson was very effective.

REFLECTIVE COMMENTS FROM DEBBIE

Stacey presented a lesson that introduced the concept of grams and kilograms and through the use of a variety of objects and hands-on activities, showed when it was appropriate to measure weight in each unit. I realize that what made it so effective was not just her use of concrete objects, not just the hands-on activities, not just her enthusiasm; it was her ability to COMBINE ALL OF THESE ELEMENTS and to PRESENT THE LESSON FROM THE STUDENT'S VIEWPOINT. It was as though she had moved to the "other side of the desk" and was looking at the subject through the eyes of a child. *She selected a colorful balance scale that looked more like a child's toy than an instrument for measurement of weight. She let the children pick objects, sight unseen, from the "Mystery Bag" instead of having the objects to be weighed already on the table. She gave each member of the 3-or 5-person groups a specific role in the weighing activity, so that each felt a sense of ownership in the group's procedures and findings. The students were motivated, they had fun, and most importantly, they learned a difficult, abstract concept at the same time.*

In addition to considering the student's viewpoint when preparing the lesson, I learned from this experience the IMPORTANCE OF KEEPING THE CHILDREN DIRECTLY INVOLVED with some task DURING THE ENTIRE LESSON, *particularly when my attention must be directed elsewhere. While Stacey was working with each small group as they weighed their bag of beans, the rest of the class had no activity on which to focus, resulting in behavior that was disruptive to Stacey and the group she was with at the time. Although the students were supposed to be observing each group while they weighed their beans, there evidently was not a direct enough involvement to maintain individual interest.*

Focusing on these two aspects in the planning stages of MY OWN FUTURE LESSONS should result in my being a more aware and creative teacher. I feel it will also make the difference between a lesson in which "I TEACH" the materials and a lesson in which the "STUDENTS LEARN" the material.

STACEY'S REFLECTIVE DECISIONS

In the future, given the chance to teach my topic again, I would definitely make several changes. In the beginning of my lesson, I had a lot of class participation, but as I went into my activity, the children could not be involved all at once.

Next time I would design a different activity SO THAT EVERY CHILD COULD BE INVOLVED AT THE SAME TIME. As a result of this change, more students are likely to remain attentive. Also, I would explain the activity before handing each group a bag of beans. Then the children would pay attention to me rather than to the beans. *What I want to do is to keep the students moti-vated, attentive, and actively involved.*

I should have used a different approach to weighing the beans. *When the children had the gram blocks, it took them a while to decide how many blocks they should put in the balance. As a result,* my lesson suffered from a waste of time. *Next time, I will have some objects, of known weights, from which they can choose. Another way that I might have better organization is to list the objects and their weights on a chart. This would give the students a source to refer to when choosing objects to place on the balance with the beans. Finally, I should have discussed the spring scale with the balance scale ahead of time instead of waiting until the children began to weigh their beans.*

STUDENT GROWTH IN REFLECTIVE INSIGHT

Debbie and Stacey entered this experience with questioning and skepticism. They questioned whether or not they knew enough about teaching to recognize the subtle interactions that occur during every teaching event. They were skeptical about understanding their observations and about telling a peer what to do or what not to do. The question was raised, "Who am I to tell another student how to improve her teaching?" These concerns were assuaged as they involved themselves personally with each other's teaching.

Not only did Debbie bring up several good points, queries, and suggestions but also Stacey presented her own questions during the conference.

Stacey showed concern about each group's motivation and interest during the hands-on activity. She was already reflecting upon the process WHILE IT WAS OCCURRING before her eyes. This demonstrated that "as teaching was in progress," Stacey was "looking into" what was happening within each group.

Stacey also showed concern regarding the students' understanding of the use of the spring scale. She realized, when problems arose while using the scale, that she had forgotten to instruct them in its use. She blamed this oversight on too much going on.

Another aspect that Stacey identified was the need to control student excitement by planning for smooth transitions between instruction and active student participation.

Stacey's "Reflective Decisions" statement further demonstrated gained insight through reflection and useful application to future lessons. As she continued to teach through the semester, we noticed deliberate attempts to address each concern here. She grew to be an exceptional planner, producing well-thought-out instructional strategies and activities with great control and smooth transitions. Stacey grew in understanding about the "act of teaching."

Debbie

While Debbie was watching the lesson in progress, she was noting several aspects of student/teacher interactions that could be applied to her own teaching. She picked up some motivational techniques used by Stacey, and she identified some oversights that led to student restlessness and inattentiveness for a while.

Being able to "look in" as a silent observer, Debbie was able later to offer helpful suggestions to Stacey. It is easier to see what changes need to be made when you aren't the one responsible for keeping everything going at once. Notice the suggestions that Debbie offered in the "Polish" section of the Peer Coaching Form.

In Debbie's "Reflective Comments," she focused on important aspects of teaching that are helpful for her own future planning as well as Stacey's. She realized the need to combine several elements at once, to anticipate the young students' viewpoints, and to keep each child actively involved during the entire lesson.

Both student teachers demonstrated the value of having a peer share in the teaching experience. They grew individually, and they grew together in insights about the act of the teaching and learning process; finally they enjoyed having a friend's input and encouragement.

PEER COACHING FORM

Teacher: Stacey   Coach: Debbie

PRAISE

1. Your use of a variety of actual objects (the balance, spring scale, coins, beans, dictionary, marker, etc.) plus the hands-on activity of each group weighing the beans, were effective ways of helping the students to grasp an abstract concept such as weight. They probably were not familiar with metric weight.

2. The way in which you let the children pick the objects from the mystery bag, rather than having them preselected by you, was a clever way of keeping them actively involved in the lesson. It helped to maintain their interest at a high level.

3. Your manner of correcting the children who were misbehaving during the discussion phase of the lesson, by calmly saying just a few words and immediately continuing with your explanation, was very effective.

   Not only did it resolve the immediate problem of the misbehavior but also the flow of your lesson was not interrupted at all. You were able to avoid losing the attention of the other students.

QUESTION

1. Concerning the objects which the students picked from the mystery bag, had you intentionally selected objects whose weights would balance?

2. Why did you introduce only the balance scale at the beginning of the lesson and wait to introduce the spring scale at a later time?

POLISH

1. Might the lesson have flowed a bit more smoothly if you had fully explained the group activity prior to passing out the beans to each group; or by withholding the beans until each group came up to use the balance?

2. Do you think you might have tried some way to keep the rest of the class involved as each group was weighing its bag of beans—perhaps recording each group's predictions of the weight of each bag, or hav-

ing the groups make comparisons among the bags? Would some activity in which each group maintained an interest in every other group's beans have prevented the inattention and misbehavior?

3. Do you think that having a list of common objects with their weights listed would have helped the children to determine the number of grams or kilograms needed to balance their beans? In that way, the students could make a more concrete comparison before dealing with the abstract concept of weight.

SKILL APPLICATION FORM

Teacher: Stacey
Coach: Debbie
Skill Focus: Balanced Participation throughout the Class

QUESTION #	VOLUNTEERS	STUDENT
Does anyone know what metric means?	2	Scott
What other units are on the meter stick?	4	Kathy
What is a scale?	5	Missy Heather Cathy
How do you weigh things?	1	Jeff
What does weigh mean?	1	Chris
What happens when something is placed in the balance?	3	Steven
What objects do you think are in the bag?	8	Michelle
Why do we weigh the book in kilograms?	4	Jeff
Should the quarter weigh 25 grams?	3	Shannon

NOTE: VOLUNTEERS—number of students who raised hands.
                  STUDENT—the student who answered.

COMMENTS: Of 22 students in the class, 11 different students were called on to answer a question during the discussion portion of the lesson. All students were actively involved.

MATHEMATICS LESSON PLAN

Stacey   Topic: Metrics

Grade Level: 2

LESSON OBJECTIVE

Following the introduction of grams and kilograms, the students will be able to use their knowledge of how to measure these weights by weighing several different objects.

SETTING FOCUS

Using the knowledge that children have about weight, they will identify objects and demonstrate their ability to weigh them on either the balance or the spring scale.

INSTRUCTION

MATERIALS

- Balance and spring scales
- 1-kilogram weight
- Gram blocks of 5, 10, and 20 gram weights
- Mystery bag containing a sponge, paper clip, quarter, marker, dime, nickel, and chalk.
- Book and sentence strips
- New vocabulary words (gram, kilogram, scale, weigh)

TEACHING STRATEGIES

Pass the 1-gram weight for the students to feel the weight. Display lightweight objects, such as erasers and crayons, and have the children guess whether they weigh the same as, more than, or less than one gram. Discuss how they can use the balance scale to check their guesses and let the students do so. Use the same procedure using the one kilogram weight and the bags of beans.

Provide bags of beans, each weighing a different amount. Let each group of students bring their bag up and decide whether they need to use the balance or the spring scale. If the children use the balance scale, they will place the beans in one tray and determine how many grams, using the block weights, will balance with it.

MODELING

Use everyday objects for students to visualize and weigh.

Guide students through weighing of the objects and the beans.

MONITOR AND ADJUST

Throughout my discussion and activities, I shall use questioning to make sure that students understand the concepts and the activities. Each concept will be reviewed.

SUPERVISED PRACTICE

Each group will come to the front of the room to weigh their bag of beans. I will observe and help students when necessary.

CLOSURE

Discuss what we learned from each activity.

1. Compare the gram and the kilogram

2. Discuss the process of weighing objects.

3. Discuss some problems encountered when weighing objects.

EVALUATION

Students will use objects and the balance or spring scale to complete math problems on an assigned workbook page.

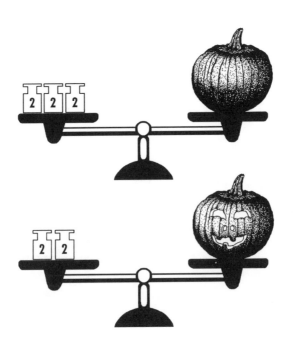

PEER COACHING SCENARIO #2
COLLEEN AND TERESA: MOTIVATION

In this teaching/coaching event, Teresa is the teacher; Colleen is the coach.

A science lesson was delivered to third-graders. See the lesson plan on p. 40, below.

Teresa was concerned about motivating her students. She thought that the topic, "properties of air," would be very abstract for third-graders and that she would find motivating them to be a problem. Based on this concern, Colleen was asked to pay close attention to motivation.

Statements of reflection and insight will be italicized in the reflective summaries.

CONFERENCE DIALOGUE

COLLEEN   It was a good idea to begin the lesson with a discussion about the difference between substances and objects. I like the example of the chalkboard eraser being the object and the felt being the substance that makes up the eraser.

TERESA   That idea came from our science class. It helped me to understand the difference, so I thought it would help them, also.

COLLEEN   The participation activity at the beginning of the lesson stimulated interest and motivation. When you had the students look around the room for examples of substances, their expressions and responses showed that they were really with you.

TERESA   Thanks. I was trying to think of how to start it off, so I decided to have them look for samples.

COLLEEN   The demonstration with the box and the bag was an excellent idea to introduce the concept of "air" as being a substance, though invisible. I heard one student say, "WOW!"

TERESA   Yes, I thought that having them focus on the box and the bags would help them understand that air is in the box. I think it is easier for third-graders to "see" that air is in a box than to see that air is in the room.

COLLEEN   The activity of going around the room to collect air was a MOTI-VATIONAL TECHNIQUE. Do you think you could have given them more direction as to where to get the air, and set some kind of limit?

TERESA   I wanted them to choose for themselves where to get it. I should have split the students up and told them to go to different parts of the room. The time limit is definitely something I should have stated. Now, when I think about it, experienced teachers seem to do that.

COLLEEN   Maybe your next lesson could have some kind of time limit on it so that you can see if it will work for you with these children.

TERESA   Yes. I was just realizing that during the activity, I could give the children something to do and tell them the time limit.

COLLEEN   The way you got the children to learn the characteristics of air offered interesting activities to help them learn, but there was a lot of confusion. Why did you choose those group activities? Can you think of other activities for the students? Do you think the students would have been less excitable if the lesson had been more structured?

TERESA   It seems that the students are better behaved when you are up there asking questions and doing demonstrations, but I think they learn more with their own materials. I need to work on ways to control them while they are working with materials, though.

COLLEEN   With hands-on activities, the children will participate more and be motivated to learn. You did a great job with that.

TERESA   Thanks. The suggestions that you gave me will be helpful for other lessons.

REFLECTIVE COMMENTS FROM COLLEEN

Teresa's presentation of her lesson on air went very well. As I was observing the lesson, I was impressed with her teaching style and the ideas that she had for the lesson.

Teresa did a few teacher demonstrations that got the students motivated to watch and learn. *I think it is an excellent idea to use as many visuals as possible so that children can actually see what is happening.*

During the lesson, the students did several activities with a clear, plastic bag to discover the characteristics of air. *These hands-on learning activities worked well because the children were highly motivated to learn.* I used this activity with the third-grade class that I have, and it worked beautifully.

There were a couple of things that I learned from observing Teresa that will help me with my lessons. *One is to make sure that I give clear directions to students* whenever they are doing a hands-on experiment. I noticed that when the children did not know what to do, there was a lot of confusion in the classroom. Also, *children need to be given time limits whenever doing things on their own,* or else they will either take too much time or get off task.

TERESA'S REFLECTIVE DECISIONS

I was nervous about my first hands-on science lesson with these students. Having an observer made me a little more nervous.

As I expected, the students got a little too rowdy when they used the materials, but they grasped the concepts quickly.

As I said, *I was nervous. Of course, the students picked up on this.* As I get more comfortable with them, I should improve. Confidence will help my ability to discipline.

I did not give enough instructions when I sent the children to "collect air." Like Colleen suggested, sending groups to different parts of the room probably would have helped. *I also should have given them a time limit.* As it was, they started "goofing off" with the bags before returning to their seats.

When I watch experienced teachers, I notice that they always give these kinds of directions. *When you are not so experienced, it is hard to remember everything all at once.* After a while, it will become a habit.

STUDENT GROWTH IN REFLECTIVE INSIGHT

Initially Teresa was very concerned about the experience. This is noted in her "Reflective Decisions" statement when she voiced concern about being so nervous.

During the debriefing conference, Teresa showed that she tried to think about how she herself learns in order to make instructional decisions to help children learn. She used an activity that had been demonstrated in a college course on campus.

The hands-on activities discussed during the conference can be further clarified by looking at Teresa's lesson plan under "Teaching Strategies, B-1." She attempted to provide a visible representation of the invisible, air.

Colleen noted that Teresa did provide motivation for the students; however, she suggested structuring the activity of collecting air. Teresa realized that setting a time and space limit is essential in such activities.

As noted during the conference, Teresa opted to have the students actively involved rather than passively seated, answering teacher-posed questions. This was her judgment as to the best way to help students work to construct meaning on their own terms. She did, however, realize that when planning future hands-on experiences, she will need to include a management system for smooth delivery.

In Colleen's "Reflective Comments," she picked up some useful tips from observing this lesson. Colleen noted evidence that young children need to have visual representations of abstract concepts in order to grasp the ideas presented. She realized that clarity of directions is an essential element to motivate children, while keeping them mentally engaged with the task at hand.

PEER COACHING FORM

Teacher: Teresa   Coach: Colleen

PRAISE

1. The discussion of objects and materials was a good way to start the lesson. The example of the eraser and the felt helped to clarify the difference between an object and the substance that makes up that object.

2. The demonstration with the big box and the plastic bag helped the children to see that air is inside the box.

3. The activity of collecting air around the room really got the children excited and interested in learning about air.

4. All the activities that the students did with the air in the bag demonstrated that air is colorless, tasteless, odorless, and that it has weight and takes up space.

QUESTION

1. What do you think you could have done to get the children to go to different areas to collect the air?

2. Do you think you ought to have given them a time limit before they went to collect the air?

3. Was there anything you could have done to make your lesson or the activities more interesting to the students?

POLISH

1. Do you think that you ought to have told the students that they would be scientists and use the clear bag to figure out the characteristics of air?

SCIENCE LESSON PLAN

Teresa   Topic: Air

Grade Level: 3

LESSON OBJECTIVE

At the end of this lesson, the learner will be able to solve a five-question puzzle on the properties of air.

SETTING FOCUS

The students will be asked to identify materials around the room. The difference between substance and objects will be explained. (An eraser is an object, felt is the substance.)

INSTRUCTION

MATERIALS

- 24 plastic bags and twist ties
- 24 party blowers
- Cardboard box
- String meter stick
- 2 balloons
- Pin
- Transparency

TEACHING STRATEGIES

Show an empty cardboard box. What is in this box? (Nothing) Do you think that something invisible might be in the box?

Give each student a bag and have everyone go to different parts of the room to collect air. To do this, students must open the bag, make a scooping motion downward, and then twist the bag shut. The air will puff-out the bag. Ask the students where they got the air. Have them close the bags with twist ties. How does the air feel? Can you see through the bag? Have them look through the bags at each other. Does it have a smell? Can you taste it? Can it support weight? (Use poker chips on the page.) What is the shape of the air in the bag? (It takes the shape of its container.) After seeing this, what do you think was in the box? (Air)

Give everyone a party blower to insert in the bag. Have them hold the opening tight around the blower and squeeze the bag. What happened to the blower? Why do you think this happened? What does this tell us? (There was air in the bag.)

Have them describe the properties of air (colorless, odorless, tasteless).

Using a transparency, have the students "identify" the components of air. Stress that it is a mixture of different gases, not one pure gas (oxygen).

MODELING

Show two balloons attached to a balance scale. What is inside each balloon? (Air) What will happen if air is removed from one of them? (Accept all predictions.)

Burst one balloon. Why did that balloon swing downward? (It weighed more.) What property of air was shown by this experiment? (Air has weight.)

Put the definition of "matter" on the board. (Matter is anything that takes up space and has weight.) Is air matter? (Yes) How do you know? (It takes up space and has weight.)

MONITOR AND ADJUST

While students are doing the puzzle, walk around to make sure that everyone is able to succeed. If not, remind them of the experiments and what they learned.

SUPERVISED PRACTICE

Complete a crossword puzzle.

CLOSURE

Go over the puzzles with the class. Discuss the properties of air.

OPTIONS

Have students draw on balloons and inflate them to observe what happens to the drawings. Weigh other objects with the balance scale (beach ball, inflated toys).

RESULTS

Everyone seemed to catch on quickly to the concepts. The whole class aced the puzzle.

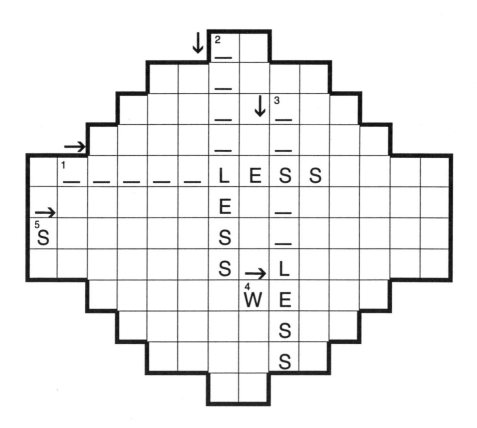

PEER COACHING SCENARIO #3
MICHELE AND SHARON: CLARITY OF DIRECTIONS

Michele and Sharon were peer coaching partners during a first-grade classroom experience. Michele is the coach; Sharon the teacher.

During the planning phase, Sharon asked Michele to watch for "clarity of directions" given to the students. This lesson was presented to first-graders early in the school year. Note the several references to the students' inability to listen and to concentrate long enough to follow the directions.

Michele selected a different style in which to present the debriefing conference. She set up the dialogue by delineating the conversation under the Peer Coaching Form elements: Praise, Question, and Polish.

Statements of reflection or insight will be italicized in reflective summaries.

PRAISE

MICHELE   I'll start off with some praises that I have for you. First, let me tell you, your handwriting did look like clear first-grade letters. I know you were worried about that.

SHARON   Good! I'm relieved to hear that.

MICHELE   Your directions were direct, specific, and seemed to be well-understood by the students. Your steps were simple and given one at a time, so the students were able to follow them very well. The poem that you read was a good motivator because it contained many words that begin with the letter "n" which was the first letter that you presented. That was a great idea! I liked the way that you gave your instruction and then asked the students to repeat it to you. For example, you said, "We start on the broken line"; then you said, "What line do we start on?" They repeated, "On the broken line." That got through to anyone who was having difficulty or was not paying attention.

SHARON   Did it really, though? Because, some people were still on the solid line and I missed seeing that.

MICHELE   Yes, it did help. William was rocking on the chair until he heard the whole class say, "On the broken line." Then, he started writing on the broken line. If you had not had the class repeat the directions back to you, William probably would not have known what to do.

SHARON   I guess that did help.

MICHELE   I loved the way you went around the room to each student and gave them individual help and praise. At first, I had written down here as one of my questions, "How will you be able to tell that each student is practicing correctly?" I had to cross it off because you monitored their work on a one-to-one basis. I also anticipated another question..."Could you have incorporated the sounds of letters into your lesson?" But then, you did that also. I like the way that you let the students who were doing a good job show off their work. They held their papers up and the other students could see them. And, you did a good job getting the students to review the lesson they had learned. At the end of the lesson, you asked the students, "What did we learn today?" This way, what they had learned was reinforced in their minds. That was super! You also let a few students get actively involved by coming up to the board to write the letters "n" or "m." That gave them the chance to demonstrate their abilities in handwriting. And, it was a great idea to let students answer other students' questions. When one student asked a question, you turned to the class and allowed the class to respond. I know this is a lot of praise, but you did a lot of things very well!

SHARON   Thank you. I didn't think it was going that well. Every time that a student asked the same question, I thought that I had caused some confusion.

MICHELE   You also made sure that each student was practicing correctly by monitoring and supervising their handwriting process and product.

SHARON   For the first lesson, I guess that things went along better than I had expected. These students are not used to listening to me for directions. So, I tried to keep them working with me by involving them directly. I'm glad that it worked.

MICHELE   Yes, I know what you mean.

QUESTION

MICHELE Did they have previous experience writing the letters "n" and "m?"

SHARON Just in whole-words that contain those letters; not in isolated letters. I thought it unusual that the students could write the word "handwriting," which contains 2 "n's", but when I asked them to write a row of the letter, they had a little trouble.

MICHELE They may not have understood what you meant when you were demonstrating writing the single letter on the board, when you verbalized the strokes as you wrote the letter.

I don't know if they could see what you meant because as you were writing, your hand covered the letter. Do you think it might have helped if you had a bigger place on the chalkboard instead of the paper so that they could see the letter while you were drawing each stroke?

SHARON One of the reasons that I used the paper was because the paper was the same size as theirs and they were used to doing it that way. Maybe I could have drawn the letters in steps, one line at a time.

MICHELE Yes, then move away after each step so that they could see each stroke formed.

SHARON I tried that with the letter "m" after they were having trouble. I couldn't understand why they had trouble writing the "m" after being able to write the "n." Why couldn't they write the "m?"

MICHELE Could you have used a silly association with the letter? For example, one humpback for the "n" letter and two humpbacks for the "m" letter. Something was needed to differentiate between them.

SHARON After the lesson, I thought about using a one-hump camel for an example of the "n" and a two-hump camel for an example of the "m."

MICHELE How could you have handled the noise level between directions? Some students were finished before the others, and it seemed that as soon as they finished, they started talking UNTIL you gave another direction. When you gave another direction, they would stop talking and listen.

SHARON   There are always students who are going to be finished before the others. I kept thinking, what could I tell these students to do? I guess I could have written the word "nine" on the board for them to write for practice.

MICHELE Sure. That would be great. It is hard to think of everything you might have to do, especially since this was your first lesson.

POLISH

MICHELE Do you think that it might have been motivating for them if you had pointed out students' names with the letters "n" or "m" in them? Then, the students could have listened for sounds in their names.

SHARON   That is a good idea! It was odd though, some students who had an "n" or "m" in their names were having trouble writing the letters in isolation, but on the bottom of the paper, they could write the letter in their names as clear as day.

MICHELE It seemed that at the end of the lesson, the students were restless. Could you have had one or two students collect the papers instead of you doing it, and then you could be getting them ready for the next part of the lesson?

SHARON   I definitely would have done that, but I thought that their teacher was going to take them to gym.

MICHEL   I see. The focus that you told me to watch for was "clarity of directions." You were very clear in your directions. The things to work on would be to let the students see the steps as you write the letters, and to attach some silly association to them to aid memory.

SHARON   Sometimes when you are explaining something to them, you think that it is clear.

MICHELE Yes, and sometimes it can be clear to one student and not to another.

SHARON   You have to tell first-graders everything. I told them to put their homework in their folders for tonight. I "assumed" that they would then put the folders back into the desks. They waited for me to tell them to do so.

MICHELE They did seem to expect that, and you did give them very clear and specific directions. I think that is why, when they finished writing and you weren't giving any other direction, they went off-task. As soon as you gave another direction, they listened. I'm sure the next time you will have extra words for the students who finish early.

SHARON   Yes, I certainly will. Thanks.

REFLECTIVE COMMENTS FROM MICHELE

As I observed my partner's lesson, I noticed many wonderful techniques. I saw how students responded to things she said and did. This was extremely beneficial to me, for I could truly understand why the students responded as they did throughout the lesson. By being the observer, I could help my partner decide on which techniques worked and which ones needed improvement. *I learned many things from the techniques that worked, and I learned just as much from things that needed improvement.*

My partner was very clear, direct, and specific during her lesson. She even had the students repeat the directions back to her to enhance the clarity further. *I realized that it's important to be clear, especially when working with first-graders.* My partner started out the lesson with a poem for motivation. I was able to see that this prepared the students and got them focused on the lesson. *Another thing that I learned is the importance of supervising to make sure that the students are practicing correctly.*

I learned that students are very interested in one another's work. My partner had a few students hold their papers up to show the rest of the class. She also had a few more students demonstrate their handwriting ability on the board. *Another interesting technique I learned was to let the students answer other students' questions.* This technique worked wonderfully in her lesson. Students were eager to help one another.

There were a few students who finished their work early and, therefore, went off-task. *I realized that a teacher always needs to be prepared to give quick students some related extra activity to keep them on-task. I also learned that a teacher needs to be able to explain a concept in as many ways as possible so that every student understands.*

By being an observer, I was able to inform my partner of many things that she may not have known otherwise, things that I may not have known otherwise, too.

SHARON'S REFLECTIVE DECISIONS

When I first realized I'd be teaching handwriting for my first peer-coaching observation, I was a little reluctant because it didn't seem like a good lesson. *Now I know I was wrong because the focus on clarity made me look at this in a different way.* This was a good lesson for clarity to be analyzed.

Handwriting is important, especially at the first-grade level. *I realized that the students would model my examples and, therefore, these examples had to be clear.* Since this was my first lesson of this nature, I put in a lot of practice and it paid off. Michele said that the lesson was clear and well understood by the class.

The next time I teach handwriting, I have to focus on activities for students who finish quickly. I've thought about letter recognition games for them, and also I've decided to have these students write additional words containing the letters that are being studied. This will provide additional enrichment and functional practice. I also have to be able to monitor the entire class's progress quickly so that I can make any necessary alterations in my demonstration.

A lesson I had thought would not be good for peer coaching turned out to be a good experience for me. We were able to expand on other activities for the students and to focus on my ability to teach lessons clearly.

PEER COACHING FORM

Teacher: Sharon   Coach: Michele

PRAISE

1. Your directions were direct, specific, and seemed to be well understood by the students. And, you gave the steps one-by-one, which resulted in clarity.

2. The poem you read contained many words that began with the first letter of study, "n." This was a good way to focus students' attention on the lesson.

3. Having the students repeat your instruction was a good way to get them to reinforce the new concepts.

4. Letting the students answer one another's questions further helped them to internalize new information.

5. When you allowed students to show off their good work, they were very enthusiastic and proud. Also, getting students to write on the board demonstrated their handwriting abilities.

6. You made sure that each student was practicing writing correctly by monitoring and supervising their handwriting process and product.

QUESTION

1. Did the students have previous experience with writing the letters "n" and "m?'"

2. How might you have praised the good listeners to get the other children to pay more attention?

3. As the children completed each step, they chattered until the next directions were given. How might you have handled the noise level between times of giving directions?

POLISH

1. Do you think it might have been more motivating if you had pointed out children's names that contained the letters "n" or "m?"

2. Do you think that if you had made the letters larger on the board, the students could have seen the directions your hand moved for each stroke?

3. At the end of the lesson, the children got out of hand. Could you have had one of the students collect the papers so that you could get the students ready for whatever was coming next?

HANDWRITING LESSON PLAN

Sharon   Topic: n & m
Grade Level: 1

LESSON OBJECTIVE

At the end of this lesson, the students will be able to write the letters "n" and "m" correctly.

SETTING FOCUS

A poem containing words that start with the letter "n" will be read to the class. Each word beginning with the sound of "n" will be discussed.

INSTRUCTION

MATERIALS

- Markers
- Oversized lined paper
- Teacher's Edition of Handwriting Text
- Chalkboard

TEACHING STRATEGIES

Demonstrate the proper way to write the letter "n." Together, with the students, write the letter "n." Walk around the room to see if everyone is writing the letter correctly. Repeat these steps as often as necessary.

Have students write the letter "n," spacing between each letter with a finger. Monitor and help any students who are having difficulty. Repeat these steps with the letter "m."

CLOSURE

Summarize the lesson by asking students what they learned. Everyone can display agreement or disagreement by holding their thumbs up or down. One or two students can come up to the board to demonstrate writing "n" and "m."

EVALUATION

Students will be given a writing sheet to practice writing the letters "n" and "m."

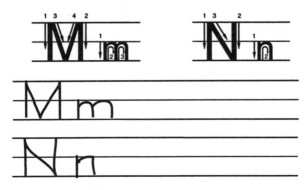

STUDENT GROWTH IN REFLECTIVE INSIGHT

It is interesting to follow Sharon's pattern of thought. You see here a very hesitant young novice who did not expect anything to be gained by this peer coaching experience. She voiced concern about having a handwriting lesson observed, assuming that not much could be seen merely in watching first-graders learn to write. Sharon's statement about her reflective decisions, however, reveals a change of heart. She said, "Now, I know I was wrong because the focus of clarity made me look at this in a different way."

During the debriefing conference, statements of doubt surfaced several times, but flickering of light also sparked. Sharon began to "see" student difficulties in light of their varied abilities and needs. She used what she observed "while teaching" to adapt instruction and to keep the students actively engaged and motivated, individually and collectively. Also, from the conference, Sharon made constructive decisions that affected future lessons positively.

Early in the conference, Michele demonstrated phenomenal insight and support for Sharon. She identified effective strategies that Sharon was using and gave her many choice suggestions to add to their repertoire. We see that Michele formulated helpful statements about student/teacher interactions and responses that occur during any lesson. She pointed out quite astutely that Sharon needed greater clarity, specificity, and continual monitoring of student success.

Both student teachers analyzed techniques and activities that were demonstrated during delivery of the lesson. They identified effective practices that broadened their cognizance of the intricacies of the act of teaching. As a result, subsequent lessons by these two budding student teachers reflected application of the suggestions that were evident during the debriefing conference.

PEER COACHING SCENARIO #4
CARMELA AND KATHY:
EFFECTIVE LESSON DELIVERY

Carmela and Kathy shared the peer coaching assignment while working in a second-grade class. Carmela acted as the coach, while Kathy was the teacher. A math lesson was delivered to this class. See the lesson plan on p. 62, below.

The lesson shown here is the second coaching session that these two student teachers shared. Kathy had not had a positive experience before, so she entered this second lesson with no expectation of salvaging her self-confidence as a teacher. When I observed her teaching during the semester, however, she nevertheless demonstrated an adequate grasp of theory and application. A wall of anxiety blocked the way between Kathy's intellectual grasp of her tasks and her emotional ability to perform. It took this experience with a peer to break through Kathy's self-imposed blockade as she overcame her lack of confidence in this area.

Kathy asked Carmela to analyze her lesson for "effective delivery." She knew that she could "write" a good lesson, but she doubted that it came across effectively to the children. She found herself so preoccupied with the how-to of teaching that she was afraid that she would fail to meet all of the needs of her students. This preservice teacher was an extremely conscientious, serious student of her profession. She wanted nothing more than to be a good teacher "for her students."

Statements of reflection or insight will be italicized in reflective summaries.

CONFERENCE DIALOGUE

CARMELA I think that you did a very good job, Kathy. The children were probably restless because it was late in the day. You had it all together from the beginning, when you announced, "It's MATH time!" They all got excited.

KATHY I didn't expect them to be that way. They really DID get excited.

CARMELA It was the way you said it—with the kind of enthusiasm that transferred over to them. I liked the use of cooperative learning, especially after our workshop today. Dividing them into groups by pre-assigned numbers was an organized way of establishing cooperative groups, and using numeral response cards during the warm-up drill elicited response from every pupil. It was quite effective when you told them to lay out their manipulative links on the desk and stated "like Cheryl is doing." This not only illustrated what you wanted them to do but also gave recognition to a student who was following directions in the process. Also, I liked the way that you told them to put their hands on their heads for a signal that they were finished. This kept them from playing with the links, which was so tempting.

KATHY   I just wish they all would have done it. There were some who never do.

CARMELA   Once again, that was not your fault. They were restless. Like I said before, the response cards were very effective. Telling the students NOT to raise their cards until you snapped your fingers was a great idea. It made them think out their answers more thoroughly. While you were waiting for them to figure out the answers, do you think it would have been of any help to write the problems on the board? They would have an example to refer back to in case they had forgotten what you said.

KATHY   Well, I wanted to stress their listening skills because they do math visually on the board all of the time. It seemed to work well.

CARMELA   It did! I was just wondering if you had given it any thought. When Dana came in late, I liked the way you took a moment to ask her neighbor if she would be a good teacher and show Dana what you were doing. When they were involved with the linking activity, you kept saying "join" and "link." Did you purposely avoid saying ADD this amount to the previous amount, until the end of the lesson?

KATHY   I wasn't sure. I asked my teacher if I should talk about addition as joining of sets, and she said that she wasn't sure if they would understand that. The whole time I was teaching, I was thinking about two sets of objects (links) being joined by linking them together. For example: You have a set of 6 links and a set of 7 links. Push them together (join) and link the sets to make one big set. Count all of the links. Instead of separate sets of 6 and 7, you have one set of 13 links together.

I neglected to say ADD because I was so involved with the lesson and the students' behavior.

CARMELA   That happens to me also. I think that they got the concept. Also, do you think it was necessary to write everyone's answer on the board? This took up a lot of time. Would it have sufficed to ask if anyone had a different answer? Then you could correct a misunderstanding at the same time.

KATHY   That did waste time, didn't it? I'll have to watch that next time.

CARMELA   It was a good idea to get several answers from the groups and to ask them if everyone agreed. This would have been a perfect time to implement the use of "thumbs-up, thumbs-down" as a way to check agreement.

KATHY   That's true. I wish that I had though of that, then.

CARMELA   Did you notice how the others listened when you told Cheryl to come to the board and demonstrate how she got her answer?

KATHY   Yes. It also quieted them down, somewhat. I didn't know what to do next to make them get quiet. Even turning out the lights didn't work.

CARMELA   I think much of that has to do with our not being their "real" teachers. They don't see us as having authority. Do you think that you should have tried something drastic with them to quiet them down?

KATHY   What would you have done?

CARMELA   I know it would have been difficult, but maybe you could have stopped, collected all the links, and told them that their misbehavior had lost them the privilege of using them. They would realize that you were serious. After a few minutes, if they calmed down, you could pass them out again (if they agreed to behave) and continue the lesson.

KATHY   I would have felt funny doing that, but next time, I'll give it a try. It may work.

CARMELA One more point I have is that you drove home the concept of telling them to add 3 links to 4 links and count the resulting 7 links. Do you think if would have helped them if you had written the equation on the board and asked two partners to demonstrate how they would show 3+4=7?

KATHY Yes, that would have made them go through the equation and understand what the "addends" and "sum" meant.

CARMELA Overall, I thought your activities were well planned and that they effectively involved all of the students. I think the class enjoyed your lesson and learned that math can really be fun.

REFLECTIVE COMMENTS FROM CARMELA

Teaching is usually a fairly isolated profession. A teacher is the sole leader of her classroom, responsible for making all of the decisions and using her best judgment to decide how and what to teach. It has been a truly reassuring and rewarding experience to be able to serve as a coach. Kathy and I together have targeted problems, discussed our views on teaching, and arrived at solutions to these problems. In the long run, this peer sharing will give both of us a foundation of what works and how to avoid problems in our classrooms.

In this lesson, I observed some effective strategies/ideas that Kathy used. Her enthusiastic attitude from the beginning of the lesson transferred to the class. I really liked the signal she used of having the students place their hands on their heads—they were tempted to play with the links, and this move kept their hands off the links. I had also never seen anyone use response cards before this lesson. These cards contained numerals. Each child had several numeral cards. When Kathy called our an equation, the students were to "show" the card that had the correct answer. For example: Kathy said, "Show me the answer for 3 + 2." The students held up the card with a numeral "5." *Kathy had the class wait to hold up their cards until she snapped her fingers. This gave everyone extra time to think through their answers more thoroughly.*

I have used response cards with numerals and with vowels since this lesson, and my children loved it. The procedure gives the teacher instant feedback to see if the students can respond correctly.

Kathy is the one who exposed me to this idea through our coaching experience. *Kathy also demonstrated "withitness" when a child entered the classroom late. Kathy took only one minute to ask the late student's neighbor to teach the activity to the girl.* I feel this was very important because teachers face constant interruptions, but they must maximize teaching time-on-task.

A major problem during this lesson was that the class got out-of-hand. They were swinging links around and playing with them more than doing what they were supposed to be doing. Kathy tried to reprimand them verbally, and she turned out the lights several times, but nothing worked for longer than a minute. After the lesson, we had a lengthy discussion about what we could do when our classes get totally out of control. *We decided that it was difficult for us student teachers to gain the children's respect because we are not their "real" teachers.* To stop serious behavior problems, we agreed that we would need to take drastic measures. *Sometimes one simply must discontinue the activity if the children cannot handle it, no matter how much planning you put into it.*

I could really sympathize with Kathy on this issue since I had experienced similar situations. Actually, it made me feel better to know that I was not the only one who had experienced difficulties in controlling a class's behavior.

One of the most positive outcomes of this coaching session, our second, was being able to share my doubts and feelings with someone else who was not only going through similar experiences, but also had observed me and knew what I was talking about. It was comforting to find out that Kathy sometimes felt as if she had failed in teaching when her lessons did not go exactly as she had planned them. *We both have come to the realization that we cannot be superhuman and have everything go perfectly when we do become "real" teachers.* We must be the best teachers we can be, but if we don't get to cover something one day, there will always be tomorrow.

KATHY'S REFLECTIVE DECISIONS

After I taught this lesson, I felt really good. I'd started out the semester with a very negative concept about my skill as a teacher, and last week's lesson did nothing to bolster my confidence. I had been so proud of this lesson! The children had started off so enthusiastically! I felt more organized and in control of the class, and the children were listening to me as their teacher. I cannot even tell you what this lesson did for me as a "teacher." It restored the feeling that "I CAN do this!"

Even better than my enjoying the lesson was when my coach had praise for it. This was my first math lesson, and I was scared that the students would not grasp the concepts. Carmela saw many of the same things going on in the classroom that I saw. *One of the biggest problems I had during this lesson was that the children were playing with the links in ways other than I had planned.* I could think of no other way of dealing with this than telling them to stop. Carmela told me that it might have been a good idea to tell them that I would give them some time at the end of the lesson to play with the links. That was a great idea, and one that I will certainly incorporate into future lessons when toys are used as manipulatives.

Although last week's peer coaching was helpful, I think this week's was even more so. *As a team, I felt that we became more aware of our requirements as teacher and as coach.* I also think that we were not so afraid to give constructive criticism or praise to one another. When I myself thought that my lesson went well, I was afraid it might be just "in my head," but when Carmela said it was a good lesson, I thought, 'WOW! Maybe it was good!"

It is unfortunate that we cannot do more peer coaching because *I feel that it has helped me tremendously.* My supervising teacher gives me a lot of feedback on all of my lessons. *What makes peer coaching so different is that is comes from someone on my own level.* Carmela and I learned a lot from our experiences with teaching and coaching. It is ironic that when this requirement was assigned, I was somewhat skeptical of its worth, but it has developed into one of the more worthwhile assignments of all of my course.

STUDENT GROWTH IN REFLECTIVE INSIGHT

Kathy is forthright about questioning her ability as a teacher. The first peer-coaching lesson was not a good experience for her; this lesson, however, turned her around.

Carmela's positive analysis pointed out several strengths about Kathy's delivery. From this analysis, Kathy realized that enthusiasm about the subject is contagious to her students. She learned that more than enthusiasm, good organization and control are also essential to effective lesson delivery. In view of this, when she plans other active participation using toys, she will set firm standards for their use and allow time for the students to play with them.

Carmela noted some effective techniques used by Kathy that she will also employ. Having the students place their hands on their heads when finished with a task, curbed inappropriate behavior. By holding off student responses until Kathy gave a signal (snapping her fingers), sufficient "wait-time" was assured. Providing response cards so that each child could show the answer, kept Kathy informed about student understanding and success.

Another benefit is both student teachers' enthusiasm for the collegial aspect of this coaching experience. Each enjoyed this shared reflective experience.

PEER COACHING FORM

Teacher: Kathy   Coach: Carmela

PRAISE

1. You showed enthusiasm when you called the students to "mathtime."

2. Having students put their hands on their heads to let you know they are finished is a good signal.

3. Snapping your fingers as a signal for the students to show their response cards allowed sufficient wait-time.

4. Asking Cheryl to explain a problem got the class's attention.

5. You incorporated good social skills when you had the students evaluate their own behavior at the end, stating, "There is no need to giggle at others if they don't understand a problem."

QUESTION

1. Would writing problems on the board have helped them to remember better?

2. Why did you think it was necessary to write each answer on the board?

3. What responses were you expecting when you asked the class how they had been learning addition, and they told you how to "write" equations?

POLISH

1. What drastic measure could you use to stop bad behavior?

2. How could you have made them understand better how they were to use the links?

3. Would using the work "add" more often than "join" have driven the concept home better?

4. Could reversing the skill have helped the class understand addition by using the links? What if you had asked the students to "show" how they would illustrate an equation that was already written on the board?

MATH LESSON PLAN

Kathy   Topic: Addition

Grade Level: 2

LESSON OBJECTIVE

Given manipulative links, the students will be able to construct and solve addition equations for the sums of 13 and 14 with 80% accuracy.

SETTING FOCUS

Students will use numeral cards to show responses to basic math problems stated orally. Each child has cards numbered 1 -12 for their responses. For example, I will say "3 + 4 and the children will flash the "7" card.

INSTRUCTION

MATERIALS

- Manipulative links
- Chalkboard
- Numeral response cards

TEACHING STRATEGIES

Have the children read the goal on the board. Ask the children to state the ways they have learned to work addition problems. Introduce the links and show the children how they are to be used.

Assign each child a number, 1 - 5 to use to form groups. All students with the #1 will form a group; all students with the #2 will form a group, etc.

Explain that each group will be working together; that each group forms a "set." Then have them use the links to form "sets" of numbers given orally. This will establish the meaning of "set" when we use the links for addition.

Discuss addition as "joining of sets." Have students join chains of links together and count the total number of links. When they respond with the answer, write it on the board. The board should look like this:

6 links   joined to   7 links   (6+7=13)

The answer response will be "13."

Probe as to why this is so. Elicit discussion among partners. Repeat the steps many times to assure understanding.

MODELING

I shall model the use of the links, chain making, and problem solving.

MONITOR AND ADJUST

Probe for lack of understanding by asking questions and walking around to each group.

SUPERVISED PRACTICE

Have the students solve problems at the board. Encourage them, if needed, to draw pictures on the board to help solve the problems.

CLOSURE

We will play the Math House game for review. Math House 13 and Math House 14 are cardboard cutouts in house shape with numbers written on them. In pockets on the back sides of the Math Houses are numeral cards. Complete each equation by placing the appropriate numeral card in a line so that the resulting equations will equal thirteen (13) or fourteen (14).

EVALUATION

Through chalkboard activities, individual responses, and pair participation, I should be able to gauge which students retained the concepts with at least 80% accuracy.

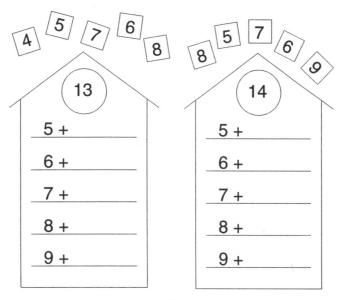

PEER COACHING SCENARIO #5
DEBBIE AND SUSAN: AUDIENCE PARTICIPATION

During this peer coaching experience, Debbie is the coach and Susan is the teacher. A math lesson was delivered to a fifth-grade class. See the lesson plan on p. 74, below.

Susan was concerned about assuring that each student be involved during the lesson. As you will note, she plans a very active lesson and one that requires critical thinking on the part of the students. She gets so "into" her teaching that she felt a need for someone else to observe the students to spot whether any students were being overlooked.

Debbie chose to present the debriefing conference in the same manner as Scenario #3, Michele and Sharon. Statements of reflections and insight will be italicized in reflective summaries.

CONFERENCE DIALOGUE

PRAISE

DEBBIE   You had a good introduction. You asked the students to define "quotient." When they did not respond, you gave a brief explanation and demonstration. I thought that using questions with division problems and asking the students to show which numeral was the quotient, was effective.

SUSAN   Thanks. I was beginning to wonder how much review would be necessary.

DEBBIE   You provided the students with good questions, and they responded with active involvement. I liked how you called on students at different tables from the beginning of the lesson.

SUSAN   Yes, I hoped that each student would participate.

DEBBIE   It is obvious that your lesson was well planned. I could almost see the lights turning on in their heads when you began to question their knowledge of quotients. Let me show you your worksheet. You had 42 responses. (See the Skill Application Form that follows.)

SUSAN   Good! They participated as I had hoped that they would.

However, it did not seem that I asked that many questions.

DEBBIE   You explained that each student would be given a calculator and that it would have to be returned. That showed your concern for their taking responsibility for the equipment. They might have just left them on the desks.

SUSAN   Some of these particular students would have tried to take them home. I always stress responsibility.

DEBBIE   You experienced very little calling-out, and you did not seem to have any problems with class control. They were all calm.

SUSAN   Actually, they are not usually like that at all. They are typically quite active. I was surprised!

DEBBIE   Are they, really? They did not show that today. Getting back to the calculators, I thought they were a good choice for this type of lesson. They will be using them throughout life.

SUSAN   Yes. They will be using calculators more and more in their daily lives. Using a calculator will be a necessary skill.

DEBBIE   You had excellent rapport with the students! I like the way you checked their answers on the calculators while walking from group to group.

SUSAN   I did not realize it at first, but they seemed to respond more as I moved around the room.

DEBBIE   Thumbs up on "thumbs-up!" This is an effective tool for locating students who may need help.

SUSAN   It also helps to reduce the noise level. I have been using this technique since the beginning of the semester, and it works!

DEBBIE   Regarding monitoring and adjusting: You were quick to respond to their problem with rounding off when they did not understand the reading on the calculator.

SUSAN   I did not know that they had not reviewed rounding off.

DEBBIE   I liked how you backed up. It seemed as if you were thinking, "Look, let's back up. You really need to know how to do this before we can proceed." I noticed that you spend a good deal of time at the board reviewing rounding off.

SUSAN   I think I should have chosen better problems. I did not even think that they would NOT have known how to round off. Because I see them only once a week, it is hard to tell what they might need.

DEBBIE   You did not choose students who were raising their hands. Good! I also liked the way that you brought the teacher and the aide into the action by letting them monitor some of the groups.

SUSAN   It gave me more opportunity to work with the smaller group that was having difficulty.

DEBBIE   The lesson was very smooth; it flowed from one topic to the next. You stated the relationships between the different types of quotient representation very well.

SUSAN   It was important that they understand numerical relationships in math.

DEBBIE   Your pacing was consistent and smooth, allowing time between topics for better understanding. You elicited responses from the students by having them restate the procedures. This was a good idea because it assessed their knowledge.

SUSAN   I wanted to make sure that each student understood.

DEBBIE   The use of the overhead was a good idea, too. Each student could follow you through the steps of problem solving.

QUESTION

DEBBIE   I have already mentioned this, but because it is the first question on the PQP Form, let's discuss it further. Have the students reviewed rounding off?

SUSAN   No. They had not had it. Mrs. R. said that they had done some work on it but that they really did not have the concept. At first, that did not sink in for me.

DEBBIE   Well, in your lesson, they received some good basics on it.

SUSAN   I would have reviewed it first, had I known. Did you see the look of shock in my eyes? I thought, "How do I do this? I did not plan for this!"

DEBBIE   You did well! You handled the situation with a quick response. What are some other ways you could use group work to help those who had problems grasping the concepts?

SUSAN   The way I was originally going to proceed with the lesson was to have them get into four groups. I was assuming that they would understand after we got through it once. The groups were going to come to the board and work together, but when I got to this point, I realized it was not going to work. At that time, I went back and changed the end of the lesson.

DEBBIE   I was thinking the same thing. You did a good job of restructuring the end of the lesson. What are some ways to handle downtime for those students who finish early?

SUSAN   That's a good question! In the past, they have come up to the teacher and asked for more problems. I could have done that, but it seemed like they were all finishing at about the same time.

DEBBIE   OK! I enjoyed your lesson, Susan.

POLISH

DEBBIE   Could you have reviewed rounding off before converting fractions to decimals?

SUSAN   Yes. I will never take that for granted again.

DEBBIE   Would there be any value to using the calculator on the overhead for a demonstration?

SUSAN   Yes. The overhead has a built-in calculator, thought I did not get a chance to practice with it before class. I could have shown them the steps for dividing fractions.

DEBBIE   Do you think that the Diamond Group would have benefitted from partner work?

SUSAN   Yes. I don't know why they were having so much trouble. They were probably too large a group; they needed to be broken down into smaller groups with fewer numbers.

DEBBIE   Although the Diamonds seemed to have the most trouble with the math, they also answered more questions than any other groups, especially toward the end. Do you think that using manipulatives would have helped some of the students?

SUSAN   Yes, it would have been helpful, but I could not think of any at that time.

DEBBIE   You were looking for audience participation. I noted that you had many group responses, and most of the students raised their hands. Most of the responses came from the seatwork, when they were using all three of the methods that you'd presented to them.

SUSAN   I reasoned that the seatwork would stimulate opportunities to participate. Even if not all of the students answered individually, at least they were part of a group.

DEBBIE   I hope that this will be useful to you.

SUSAN   Yes, it is! Thank you.

REFLECTIVE COMMENTS FROM DEBBIE

Observing a peer is quite different from observing a practicing teacher who is well versed in her lessons. Student teachers have higher expectations of the practicing teacher due to her experience. Peers have expectations of one another equivalent to their own of themselves. Peers share the same experiences in student teaching, and they are on the same level, which makes the comfort level higher. They can relate to each other about common problems.

In Susan's lesson I found some ideas for pacing lessons and monitoring classroom activity. Her lesson flowed smoothly, and much of that was due to allowing time for class participation. She was able to monitor the class by using the cooperating teacher and a parent aide as helpers. It was nice to see some things which I have been working toward in my own classroom turn out to be successful.

In addition to learning techniques from Susan's lesson, I learned some things about communication. *I learned that peer coaching is an excellent way to make use of teacher interactions.* Ours was a prime example of sharing thoughts to achieve common goals in the classroom.

SUSAN'S REFLECTIVE DECISIONS

Following the debriefing conference, Debbie discussed various positive attributes of my lesson as well as areas in which I could enrich future lessons. She liked my use of the thumbs-up technique. *Because this technique allows for a high level of participation while maintaining a low level of noise, I plan to implement it even more in the future.*

Debbie also praised my attempts at drawing responses out of the students when they had trouble answering a question. *I tried to help the students apply their own background knowledge to the problem as they moved toward the solution.* She called attention to my calling on students whose hands were not raised. In addition, I moved from table to table in my search for answers. While I was doing this subconsciously, I shall make the effort to continue to do so in the future.

Debbie told me that she was relieved when I began to check whether each student was working with a calculator to do the assigned problem. Some students were not doing the assigned problems until I began checking on them. *I will always be sure to check all students throughout the lesson in the future.*

I learned that I can "land on my feet" when something unexpected happens. I had planned to teach a lesson that required the knowledge of rounding off numbers, and I was horrified to find out that the class was not familiar with the concept. *I will ALWAYS be sure to ensure that the students have prior knowledge of concepts upon which the new lesson is based.*

Debbie told me that she liked my technique of eliciting student responses to restate the procedures that they had been taught. *We both think that this is a good way to check that the material has been learned.*

Debbie has made me more aware of my students' downtime in between activities. *She alerted me, as well, to the enormous value of using the teacher's demonstrator calculator on the overhead. This I will definitely learn how to use in the future.*

Although Debbie thought that my pace was good, I did not get to my planned seatwork. *It is obvious to me that it is more important to take time to develop new concepts than to cover a prescribed amount of material.* I will try to be very flexible during future lessons.

Even though a lesson plan might have to be changed drastically under certain circumstances, I am confident in my abilities to ad lib some part of the lesson in order to handle unforseen contingencies. *I must try to be aware (at all times) of various ways that my lesson can drift, and to be able to redirect and organize effective lessons from that point.*

STUDENT GROWTH IN REFLECTIVE INSIGHT

Debbie and Susan approached this project like veteran teachers. They seemed to have insights that would not be expected at this level of teachers in training.

Debbie noted that steady pacing throughout the lesson and monitoring student progress are important to a lesson's delivery. She experienced the value of having a peer with whom to delve into the intricacies of teaching.

Susan was an exceptionally good planner. She thoughtfully sequenced this lesson and provided numerous opportunities for students to be actively involved, using cooperative learning strategies. However, she discovered that surprises can occur, which will throw off the best preparation.

When Susan found that the students did not have a prerequisite skill, upon which the success of the new instruction rested, she filled in with additional practice, teaching them what they lacked. She discovered what she had not known about herself: that she is capable of adapting a lesson in midstream.

Susan became aware of the effective use of probing and cueing to elicit appropriate responses from the students. The students used calculators, but thanks to Debbie, her coach, Susan realized that she too could have used the overhead calculator to model correct usage.

SKILL APPLICATION FORM
OPPORTUNITY FOR AUDIENCE PARTICIPATION

Place a mark in seats whenever a student participates during the lesson.

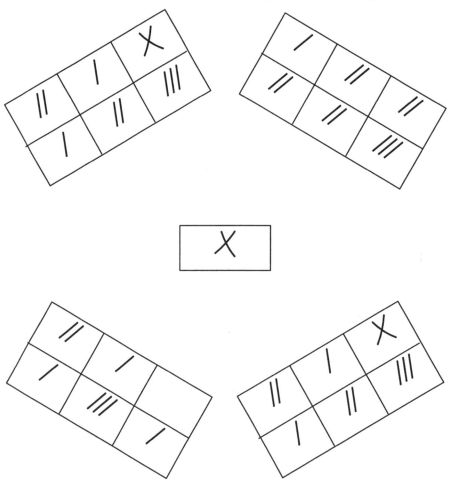

There were 42 responses during the lesson.

"X" represents students who did not respond to questions.

Most responses were given during questions related to the three methods used.

TOTAL 42

PEER COACHING FORM

Teacher: Susan   Coach: Debbie

PRAISE

1. Your introduction established focus for the students. You had them identify quotients.

2. The questioning strategies that you used elicited the active participation of all students.

3. It was a good strategy to use calculators during this lesson. You also reminded the students of their responsibilities regarding the calculators.

4. You have a good rapport with this class. There were no class-control problems.

5. Using "thumbs-up" for agreement helped you to identify students who were unsure.

6. You really landed on your feet when you discovered that the students did not have the prerequisite skill of rounding off numbers.

7. Your pacing and delivery were smooth. Concept relationships were developed, and time was allowed to aid better understanding.

QUESTION

1. Had the students reviewed rounding off of numbers before this?

2. How else could you use group work?

3. What are some ways to use downtime with students who finish early?

POLISH

1. How helpful would it be to review rounding off before converting fractions to decimals? What would you do?

2. Do you think the Diamond Group should have been divided into smaller groups? How would you accomplish this?

3. Would the use of manipulatives be appropriate for this lesson? How would you use them?

MATH LESSON PLAN

Susan   Rewriting Remainders

Grade Level: 5

LESSON OBJECTIVE

Given division problems, the students will be able to express the remainders as whole numbers, fractions, and decimals with 85% accuracy.

SETTING FOCUS

Write the division problem, 5/4 on the board, and show the remainder by circling it. Then ask students what the circled number is called. Write three more division problems on the board and have the students identify each remainder.

INSTRUCTION

MATERIALS

- Overhead projector
- Ditto
- Chalkboard
- Mini-chalkboards
- Math book
- Calculators

TEACHING STRATEGIES

One easy way to express a remainder is as a whole number. Show how to do this with the problems on the board. MAKE SURE TO KEEP THE PROBLEMS ON THE BOARD SO THAT THE CLASS CAN FOLLOW ALONG. Also, have the students do these as well at their desks.

A second way to express a remainder is as a fraction. Show how to do this with the examples on the board, and have the students do these at their desks.

Pass out calculators. "Do you remember how we can get a decimal from a fraction?" (Show 1/2 = .5)

A third way we can express a remainder is as a decimal. "To make it easier for you to figure out what the decimal is, I have provided you with calculators. Let it divide for you."

Have the students figure out the decimal values on their calculators as I do the problems with them at the chalkboard.

Pass out chalkboards and chalk/erasers. Erase all but two of the previous examples so that the students can still follow. They should also write down the problems.

Put four problems on the board. Assign one to each group, and have the students express the remainder in their division problem in all three ways: as a whole number, as a fraction, and as a decimal. Have one student from each group come to the board to do their problem.

Assign problems on p. 316 (#'s 1-5) to be done on the chalkboard and at their desks. Go over them on the overhead while orally "talking through" each step.

MODELING

Solve problems on the board while discussing each step with the class. Have the students do sample problems for their classmates.

MONITOR AND ADJUST

Mrs. R. (the teacher), the parent aide, and I will circulate during the seatwork phase of the lesson to help students when problems arise.

SUPERVISED PRACTICE

The problems for this portion of the lesson will be numbers 1-5 on page 316, to be done on the mini-chalkboards.

CLOSURE

"Now that we have practiced writing the remainders in three ways together, explain to me how this was done." As a summary of statements, ask volunteers to explain the steps to the rest of the class.

EVALUATION

Collect assigned homework for grading.

SUMMARY

These five peer coaching scenarios have enabled us, as professors of teachers-in-training, to look into their teaching samples. We are convinced that our expectations of the value of preservice peer coaching were more than realized. Students documented the usefulness of peer coaching in their "reflective comments" and "reflective decisions." Here are a few of their testimonials to the value of peer coaching:

✦ As a team, I felt we became more aware of our requirements as teacher and as coach.

✦ It is unfortunate that we cannot do more peer coaching because I feel that it has helped me tremendously.

✦ In addition to learning techniques, I learned about communication with a colleague.

✦ It has been a truly reassuring and rewarding experience to be able to serve as coach.

✦ We were able to target problems, discuss our views on teaching, and arrive at solutions together.

SAMPLE WORKSHEET

Change each fraction to a decimal.

1. $\dfrac{7}{10}$ 2. $\dfrac{16}{100}$ 3. $\dfrac{23}{1000}$

Change each decimal to a fraction.

4. 0.4   5. 0.45   6. 2.75

Choose the correct answer.

7. The decimal form of the fraction $\dfrac{5}{8}$ is:

  a. 0.58   b. 0.625   c. 0.652

8. Which of these mixed numbers is equal to 1.5?

  a. $15\dfrac{1}{2}$ b. $1\dfrac{4}{5}$ c. $1\dfrac{1}{2}$

9. Which fraction is equivalent to 0.6?

  a. $\dfrac{6}{10}$ b. $\dfrac{1}{3}$ c. $\dfrac{2}{3}$

Compare. Write <, =, or >.

10. $\dfrac{3}{5}$ _____ 0.5   11. 2.5 _____ $2\dfrac{1}{2}$

12. How much greater than 0.75 is $\dfrac{4}{5}$?

Compute.

13. $\dfrac{2}{3}$ of __?__ = 60   14. $\dfrac{3}{4}$ of __?__ = 60

15. Change $\dfrac{9}{11}$ to decimal notation.

CHAPTER 4

TRAINING FOR COACHING

In order for preservice teachers to use coaching to develop a reflective disposition towards their process of acquiring skills and applying strategies that they learned about in their college Education courses, they require systematic guidance in the techniques of coaching.

KNOWLEDGE ABOUT COACHING

To know how to coach, one must grasp the concept of coaching. As preparation for a workshop on how to implement coaching in assigned schools, we require preservice teachers to read about the use of coaching with inservice and preservice teachers. Our students read chapters 1, 2, and 3 of this text, and two Phi Delta Kappa fastbacks: #277 *Improving Teaching through Coaching* (1988), by Gloria Neubert, and #371, *Peer Coaching in Teacher Education* (1994), by Gloria Neubert and Lois Stover. The following reader-response questions are given to our students to guide their reading (use Worksheet #1 in the *New Teachers' Peer Coaching Workbook*). We then use these questions to structure our subsequent in-class introducto ry discussion of peer coaching:

1. In your own words, explain *peer coaching*.

2. What are the benefits of peer coaching? What benefit is most important to you?

3. Select one scenario reported in the readings that impressed you the most. Why did it impress you?

4. What questions do you have about peer coaching?

Skill Focus

Next, we call to the students' attention the need to focus on a single teaching skill or strategy during a coaching experience. It is unreasonable to ask a novice teacher or coach to attend to, analyze, and reflect on every aspect of a lesson. Not even veterans can adequately process the many variables operating at once in a single lesson.

We ask the preservice teachers to make an initial list of teaching skills or strategies that they would like to be coached on (use Worksheet #2 in the *New Teachers' Peer Coaching Workbook*). Drawing on their limited experience, our students typically compose a short list, but skills and strategies are added as the course and the field experience progress, and as additional skills and strategies are introduced, discussed, observed, and experienced.

Our students are then shown sample "Skill Application Forms" to assist them in concentrating on one skill for a coaching episode. Example A (p. 79) is a Skill Application Form that one inservice coaching pair designed for the coach to complete while focusing on the teacher's use of wait time in relation to the difficulty of the question.

Example B (p. 80) is a Skill Application Form that a coaching pair of college instructors designed to help one of them use less lecture and more student-centered activities over the course of a semester. We use this example to show our preservice teachers how Skill Application Forms might be used repeatedly to show change over time. Notice how teacher-centered the Instructor's lesson was in February but how it had shifted to student-centered by May.

Example C (p. 81) is a Skill Application Form that a preservice coaching pair developed for a student teacher who was attempting to increase her use of positive responses (as opposed to neutral or negative responses) to students during class discussions.

Sometimes, teachers attempt to incorporate a skill or strategy that does not lend itself to quantifying data on a Skill Application Form; therefore, the coach will take specified notes. For example, a coach completed the Skill Application Form in Example D (p. 82) while observing a teacher who was learning to use concept attainment with her students in order to foster inductive reasoning. The teacher and coach had agreed during their planning lesson that the coach would record information about the essential elements of concept attainment—the examples the teacher gave the students to examine, the prompting questions the teacher asked about the examples, and the actual generalizations the students made about the examples.

EXAMPLE A: SKILL APPLICATION FORM

SKILL FOCUS: WAIT-TIME

Teacher's Questions	Time in seconds that elapsed between asking a question and calling on a student (Stopwatch time)	Number of students who have hands raised (volunteers to answer the question)
In terms of language, how are the two fables different?	2	3
What is the purpose of using dialogue in this fable? What is the effect achieved by the author?	5	12
In the second fable, where is the "said" statement of the first sentence?	1	2
And in the second sentence?	1	7
Why do you think the author chose to split the dialogue statement in the middle	7	9 (Long pause before students began raising their hands)

EXAMPLE B: SKILL APPLICATION FORM

SKILL FOCUS: STUDENT-CENTERED INSTRUCTION

Teacher-Centered Instruction			Student-Centered Instruction	
Lecture	TQSU	TASQ	SA	TPD
February				
7 minutes				
	15 seconds			
		1) 2.6 min.		
		2) 2.5 min.		
		3) 1.6 min.		
		4) 37 sec.		
		5) 27 sec.		
		6) 20 sec.		
5.8 min.				
		18 sec.		
1 minute				
		1) 51 sec.		
		2) 35 sec.		
	10 sec.			
		2 min.		
2 min.				
		1 min.		
7.3 min.				
		1) 33 sec.		
		2) 15 sec.		
		3) 1.6 min.		
May				
			42 minutes (structured group work) 25 minutes (viewing film)	
				6 minutes

TQSU: Teacher Questioning Students for Understanding (Example: "Does anyone have a question about this law?")

TASQ: Teacher Answering Student's Questions

SA: Student Activity; teacher-assigned small group or individual work

TPD: Teacher-prompted Discussion; students expressing responses/opinions to the instructor and to each other (Example: "What does anyone think about labeling special needs students?")

EXAMPLE C: SKILL APPLICATION FORM

SKILL FOCUS: RESPONDING POSITIVELY TO STUDENTS' RESPONSES

<u>Positive Responses</u>	<u>Neutral Responses</u>	<u>Negative Responses</u>
/////	/////	/////
/////		/////
/////		/////
/////		/////
/////		/////
/////		/////
/////		
/////		

Example D: Skill Application Form

Skill Focus: Concept Attainment/Inductive Reasoning

Students examined the following examples:

Protagonists	Antagonists
Montresor	Fortunato
Harrison Bergeron	H-G Men/Diana
Margo	William and the other children

The teacher asked the following prompting questions:

What is the relationship between Montresor and Fortunato?

Between Harrison Bergeron and the H-G Men and Diana?

Between Margo and William and the other children?

What do the three people listed under "protagonist" have in common?

Are they all "good" characters? Let's check that.

Was Montresor good?

So what do all the "Protagonists" have in common?

Now what do all the "Antagonists" have in common?

The students arrived at the following generalization:

A "protagonist" is the main character in the story; not always a good person.

An "antagonist" is someone in the story who opposes the protagonist.

A standard seating chart can sometimes be an appropriate Skill Application Form. We tell our students about a teacher who was learning to use cooperative learning and was concerned about the constituency of the groups he had planned. The coach observed each group for a designated period of time and put a slash mark (/) in the appropriate student's seating chart block every time he/she contributed to the discussion. During the debriefing conference, the teacher was able to look at the Skill Application Form and determine the extent to which each student was contributing in the assigned group.

Skill Application Forms, which are designed by the teacher or cooperatively by the teacher and coach, force both to log and consider the standards of evidence (student and teacher behaviors) that signal successful or unsuccessful application of the skill and use (or disuse) of the strategy. Skill Application Forms yield the coaching pair objective data to examine and analyze during the debriefing session.

Conferences often begin with the one who taught interpreting the information first. This provides a way for teachers to objectify the aspects of their teaching that they are trying to learn about or improve, and to make conclusions about their own progress. Often the data speak for themselves, thus taking the onus off the coach for deciding if the teacher has been successful.

Example A above allowed the teacher (and coach) to see whether more wait-time resulted in more student participation, and whether the complexity of the question related to the amount of wait-time and to student participation. Example B allowed the instructor to look in on her lesson to see the amount of time she spent each class session on teacher-centered as compared to student-centered instruction. Example C comforted the preservice teacher who was concerned that she was not giving her young pupils sufficient positive responses during class discussion. Example D provided the coaching pair with a summary of the examples that the teacher used in her lesson, a record, and the order of, all the prompting questions asked, and a transcript of the final generalization stated by the students. Using the Skill Application Form, the teacher and coach were able to replay the lesson and determine the effectiveness of the teacher's prompting questions in helping students distinguish the concepts of "protagonist" and "antagonist." In the final example, the use of marks on a seating chart allowed the coaching pair to see which students were leading (or taking over) groups, and whether there were students who were not contributing at all to the discussion. Notice the two Skill Application

Forms developed and used by the preservice teachers in the examples cited in Chapter 3. (See pp. 31 and 72.)

CONFERENCING TECHNIQUES

The debriefing conference is the most crucial component of the coaching process. It is here that the lesson is reviewed, analyzed, and reflected upon by the pair of peers. We teach our preservice students to use a non-directive conferencing style that includes four types of feedback:

1) Praise Comments

2) Clarifying Questions

3) Eliciting Questions

4) Leading Questions

Praise Comments are affirmations, statements of approval, concerning *what* the teacher did well in conjunction with the skill focus, and *why* this teaching behavior was effective. Recall the conference dialogue between Staci and Daphne in Chapter 1 (pp. 9 and 10). Staci, the coach, makes several Praise Comments. In the following two examples, notice that Staci tells *what* was effective and also *why* she thought it was effective:

> *The positive reinforcement you used throughout the lesson was good. It encouraged the students to participate in the discussion.*

> *I also thought that discussing the vocabulary words before the story helped the students understand the reading material better.*

Praise Comments serve two important functions: First, they explain why some specific behavior is being praised. They link the teacher's specific behavior to a generalized reason for the effectiveness of that behavior. In the first example above, Staci is generalizing that when Daphne gives her students positive reinforcement, it encourages the students to participate in the discussion. Daphne now has heard a principle which might transfer to her future teaching.

Praise Comments also boost the fragile ego of the preservice teacher in the position of the novice. The following statements are typical of preservice teachers' reactions to the required praise component of coaching:

My partner was able to make me aware not only of my weaknesses but also of my strengths! This activity helped to raise my confidence level because its emphasis is on the positive.

I received so much assistance from my coach in understanding why things were working! It helped me feel good about myself. The praise—it felt great!!!"

Clarifying Questions are questions the coach asks because he/she does not understand something that happened during the lesson or something said during the conference. For example, Staci (p. 10) asks Daphne why she thinks the story she had the children read was included as a part of the curriculum. Apparently, Staci is puzzled about the intended purpose of this story which the students are to comprehend. Daphne responds by relating her belief in the curriculum's responsibility to develop the students' backgrounds of experience, "Because kids need a variety of sources of information about the world around them. Some children might not have the opportunity to experience things such as a circus . . . " (p. 10). If Daphne had not been able to explain the purpose of this type of story, this clarifying question might have jolted her unquestioning use of the required curriculum material.

Clarifying Questions can also result in learning for the coach. Later in her "Reflective Comments," Staci marvels at her own lack of sensitivity to this purpose:

Well, I thought everybody had been to a circus! Then I realized that there was a lot of truth in what she said. When I am teaching, I may have students that come from disadvantaged families. I must make an effort to be sensitive to these students and not make assumptions like I did while conversing with Daphne. (p. 12)

Clarifying Questions can also be used by the coach to express, indirectly, reservations about some aspect of the lesson. For example, Staci asked Daphne (p. 11), "Why did you decide to bring in library books to show the students?" Staci either did not understand the intended use of the books for the lesson she observed, or she might have had reservations about their use. Clarifying Questions require teachers to reflect on *why* they chose to do something. In answering the question, they must express a rationale for their decision.

In this case, Daphne responded that she believed that the library books " ... would be a good motivation" and that the students " ... had the chance to read them later in the day." This rationale apparently seemed satisfactory to Staci because she said she might try a similar motivational approach for her upcoming lesson. In other instances, however, when teachers have not been able to justify their practices satisfactorily, they have come to realize their inappropriateness. The following excerpt from the debriefing conference of two preservice teachers who were focusing on the use of writing-to-learn in a math class shows how the coach's Clarifying Question can help the teacher rethink a practice:

COACH: How did you feel about your decision to have the students develop flow charts on their own?

TEACHER: Some of them were really confused, weren't they? I think now it would have worked better as pairs. They could have brainstormed together.

Clarifying Questions (as well as other types of questions) can also make teachers aware of what they actually did in a lesson. For example:

COACH: Did you mean to go over the answers to the drill before you started the developmental part of the lesson?

TEACHER: I did go over the drill—didn't I? If I didn't, I meant to.

Eliciting Questions are questions the coach asks to prompt the teacher to explore alternatives or options. Staci asks Daphne to consider "other methods of guided reading" (p. 10) that she could have used in her lesson. Eliciting Questions, like Clarifying Questions, are designed to encourage the teacher to be an active learner and to reflect on choices. Eliciting questions are particularly useful in coaxing preservice teachers to recall instructional strategies they have learned about during campus course work but which they have not yet actualized in their practice. Eliciting Questions often begin with leads such as the following:

- Is there another way you might have ... ?

- Did we learn any strategies in our Curriculum course that might be appropriate for ... ?

- Is there anything you might have done differently if you were to repeat this lesson?

- How else might the students . . . ?

Leading Questions are the coach's suggestions or recommendations for improvement, stated in question form. Common leads for such questions are:

- Do you think . . . ?

- What would happen if . . . ?

- Could you have . . . ?

Staci asks Daphne, "Do you think the children would follow the story more closely if they read silently rather than out loud?" (p. 10) Staci is really saying, "I don't think all the children were paying attention. I think you should have the students read the story silently, not aloud." The difference in the effect between a Leading Question and a peremptory recommendation is noteworthy: The role of the coach is to encourage, not to command. The teacher may respond to a Leading Question actively, reflecting as a decision maker, instead of being forced into a decisive corner. The coach's Leading Questions do not express usurpation of the teacher's own control. It happens that in response to Staci's Leading Question about the silent reading, Daphne does agree with the embedded recommendation. Notice, however, that to Staci's next Leading Question ("Do you think having the kids write down the answers to the focus questions would improve comprehension?"), Daphne, who knows her students' habits better than does the coach/visitor, decides: "I think the students would tend to write down other students' answers instead of thinking for themselves, as they do in group discussion." Daphne, the teacher, appropriately maintains control of the reflective decisions for her class.

We introduce our preservice teachers to these four types of coaching feedback statements by reviewing the definitions and showing them examples of each type. The purpose of each type is also discussed.

Next, we give our students a worksheet, as shown in Example E, that includes actual examples of feedback statements given by coaches (use Worksheet #3 in the *New Teachers' Peer Coaching Workbook*). Students work in pairs on Part A to classify responses into the four categories—Praise Comments, Clarifying Questions, Eliciting Questions or Leading Questions—and to defend their choices. They then work with their partners on Part B to identify the problem with each statement and to rewrite these inappropriate conferencing responses. An all-class discussion finally takes place in which we reach consensus on all the sample statements.

EXAMPLE E: COACHING COMMENTS

PART A: Classify each of the following coaching comments as either Praise, Clarifying Question, Eliciting Question, or Leading Question.

1. What other forms of grouping could you have used to encourage more participation from the less able students?

2. The math problems the students were to solve worked well because they were sequenced from the easy to the more difficult.

3. What do you think would happen if you had given students nonexamples as well as examples of polygons?

4. Why did you chose to use a web for this writing assignment?

5. Using the two composition models—one with specific detail and one without specific detail—was excellent. I'm sure the students will remember what they learned about the effectiveness of detail because they were so involved in contrasting the two models.

6. Why did you chose not to give the students copies of the song lyrics as you had originally planned?

7. Do you think Robert would have been more cooperative if he had been part of the second group?

PART B: Rewrite the following coaching comments to make them more effective. Remember that Praise Comments should tell *what* and *why*, and all Questions should put ownership of the decision into the hands of the teacher.

1. Using a semantic web was good for these students.

2. Why did you use this awful story?

3. If I were going to teach this lesson, I would have used a directed reading approach.

4. There was too much commotion during group work. Why don't you have the students work alone for the next several classes?

PRAISE-QUESTION-POLISH (PQP) SHEET

We teach our preservice coaches to collect and organize their Praise Comments, Clarifying Questions, Eliciting Questions and Leading Questions during the observation of the lesson on a Praise-Question-Polish (PQP) sheet, as shown in Example F. The "PQP" acronym originated as a tool to facilitate response to written compositions. (See Lyons, 1981 and Neubert and McNelis, 1986.) In the original PQP, students give their peers praise (P), ask general Questions (Q) about the composition, and offer declarative statements for polishing (P), that is, changing and improving the writing. We have adapted this to use as a lesson observation instrument, have subdivided general Questions into Clarifying and Eliciting types, and have required that Polish suggestions also be in the form of questions so that ownership for change and reflective decisions remains in the hands of the teacher.

EXAMPLE F: PRAISE-QUESTION-POLISH (PQP)

COACHING

PRAISE (*What* went well and *why* it was effective)

QUESTION (Clarifying Questions—questions the coach asks because s/he does not understand; Eliciting Questions—questions the coach asks in order to have the teacher explore options for change or variety)

POLISH (Suggestions in the form of questions)

The PQP notes made by the coach while observing the lesson are then used as the basis for the debriefing conference. Below is the PQP sheet completed by Staci as she observed Daphne's lesson. Notice the parallel between these notes and the conference dialogue (pp. 9-11).

PRAISE

1) The positive reinforcement used throughout the lesson was good because it encouraged the students to participate in the discussion.

2) The discussion of the vocabulary before reading the story was helpful in understanding and reinforcing the material.

3) Having the students draw what they would look like if they were clowns was an excellent follow-up activity because it allowed the children to use their creativity and imaginations.

QUESTION

1) Eliciting: What other methods of guided reading could you have used?

2) Clarifying: Why do you think this story was included in this curriculum?

3) Clarifying: Why did you decide to bring in library books to show the students?

POLISH

1) Do you think the children would follow the story more closely if they read silently rather than out loud?

2) Do you think having the kids write down the answers to the focus questions would improve their comprehension?

During this phase of the coaching workshop, we have our preservice teachers examine several model PQP forms (such as Staci and Daphne's) that have been used by inservice teachers as well as preservice teachers in previous classes. Students also read and discuss the corresponding transcripts of audio-tapes of debriefing sessions in order to "hear" how the PQP form frames the discussion. "Listening in" on others who have gone before in this course, and recognizing the insights about teaching that can occur through coaching appears to reduce some of the anxiety associated with a critique of a peer's lesson and of receiving a peer's critique.

Upon completion of this phase of the training, our students are ready for on-campus practice in coaching.

COACHING PRACTICE

Before our preservice teaching students are required to teach and coach in the schools, they practice coaching on campus. We describe for them a teaching scenario, tell them the teacher's skill focus, give them a PQP form and corresponding Skill Application Form (if needed for the skill focus), then have them assume the role of a coach and complete the forms as they watch a videotaped mini-lesson (use Worksheet #4 in the *New Teachers' Peer Coaching Workbook*). At the end of the lesson, they meet in small groups to discuss and compare Praise Comments and the three kinds of coaching Questions. As the course continues, we also have students practice coaching in conjunction with practice lessons they teach on campus to a small group of peers. In this way, coaching becomes an integral and complementary part of the course-work and a natural follow-up to a teaching event.

COACHING PARTNER SELECTION AND PLANNING

Coaching is a personal as well as a professional activity; therefore, we warn students to think carefully about the selection of a coaching partner. Close friends may or may not feel comfortable asking reflective questions of each other. We allow students to submit names of two individuals who, they believe, could give them knowledgeable and objective feedback. In most cases, we honor student requests for coaching partners; otherwise, we use our limited acquaintance with the students to pair them, or we assign coaching partners randomly. Sometimes, assignments to cooperating schools dictate the pairings.

Once the coaching partners are paired, we talk to our students about the need for confidentiality; that is, neither the teacher nor the coach shall discuss either their peer's performance or what has been exchanged during a coaching episode outside the class and materials turned in to us. Confidentiality is necessary if the coaching relationship is to be built on trust.

We then allow time in class for the coaching partners to address the logistics of time for coaching in their assigned school. They are required to allocate time for at least two coaching experiences. Each coaching session includes the following:

1) a planning conference during which the teacher and coach agree on the skill focus of the lesson to be taught, develop the Skill Application Form (if appropriate), and overview the lesson procedure

2) observation of the preservice teacher's lesson by the coach and completion of the Skill Application Form and PQP form

3) a debriefing conference during which the coach and the teacher use the information on the two forms to guide their reflective dialogue.

The debriefing session is audio-taped and transcribed. After the debriefing conference, the teacher and coach each react to the coaching experience by writing reflective summaries. Students are asked to respond to the following questions:

"What did you learn about your teaching as a result of this coaching experience?" (Question for the Preservice Teacher)

"What did you learn about teaching as a result of serving as a coach?" (Question for the Coach)

SUMMARY

The following is an outline of the training model described in this chapter:

A. Knowledge Level

1. Discussion of the definition, phases, and benefits of coaching (Worksheet #1 in the *New Teachers' Peer Coaching Workbook*).

2. Initial listing of skills and strategies and examination of model Skill Application Forms (Worksheet #2 in the *New Teachers' Peer Coaching Workbook*).

3. Training in the recognition and writing of the four types of feedback for conferencing (Praise Comments, Clarifying Questions, Eliciting Questions, and Leading Questions) (Worksheet #3 in the *New Teachers' Peer Coaching Workbook*).

4. Examination of model PQP forms (e.g., in chapters 1 and 3).

B. Coaching Practice on Campus (Worksheet #4 in the *New Teachers' Peer Coaching Workbook*)

1. Videotaped mini-lessons

2. Practice lessons

C. Coaching Partner Selection and Planning

This training model has resulted in the effective use of peer coaching for helping preservice teachers reflect as they apply new teaching skills and strategies. The three types of questions used for conferencing discourage a disposition to expository ("telling") advice on the part of the coach. Instead, the teacher is encouraged in the active, reflective stance by being encouraged to analyze, seek alternatives, provide a rationale, and hypothesize in order to answer the coach's Clarifying, Eliciting, and Leading questions.

CHAPTER 5

REFLECTIONS ON PRESERVICE PEER COACHING

This preservice peer coaching project was designed to use coaching as a vehicle for the following:

1. moving preservice teachers from a non-reflective to a reflective stance during their initial teaching experiences

2. helping preservice teachers apply the skills they are learning about and practicing during their on-campus methodology courses;

3. encouraging a positive attitude toward collegial analysis as a means of continued professional growth

As preservice peer coaching was incorporated into the junior-year curriculum course, we asked the four following questions about our preservice coaching project to determine whether our goals had been achieved.

DEMONSTRATION OF REFLECTIVE THINKING

QUESTION #1: WOULD STUDENTS DEMONSTRATE REFLECTIVE THINKING DURING PEER COACHING?

The lesson plans, Skill Application Forms, PQP forms, transcripts of audio-recordings of the debriefing sessions and reflective summaries provided evidence that *all* the students did engage in reflective thinking during the peer coaching process.

It appears that the feedback format prompted reflection, the debriefing conferences allowed time for processing the details of the lesson, and the writing of the reflective summaries resulted in the students' articulation of pedagogical principles that could guide their future planning and teaching. For example, two students wrote:

> *I will* always *be sure that the students have prior knowledge of concepts upon which the new lesson is based.*

> *I learned the importance of keeping the children* directly *involved during the entire lesson."*

Most of these principles had been presented in their college courses. This coaching process appears to have assisted the preservice teachers in linking theory and practice in the real world of the classroom.

Most preservice teachers functioned consistently at the reflective level of "technical rationality." (See discussion Zeichner and Liston's reflective levels in Chapter I.) Although some teacher educators might find it disappointing that these students are only on this first level of reflection, we view reflection as a developmental process, and are jubilant that our junior-level, preservice teachers have moved, as a result of peer coaching, from a non-reflective stance to functioning with the depth of "technical rationality" that is demonstrated in the scenarios in Chapters 1 and 3.

Future research will be needed to determine whether modifications to the peer coaching process outlined here will result in preservice teachers' engaging in higher levels of reflection: Level two—"practical action" and Level three—"critical reflection." For example, could the coaching feedback (i.e., Praise Comments, Clarifying Questions, Eliciting Questions and Leading Questions) be modified during this field experience or during student teaching to focus the attention of teacher and coach alike on aspects and dispositions required for reflective levels two and three? Just as the questions used in this coaching experiment triggered level one reflections, could other, more-focused questions serve as catalysts for reflective thinking about assumptions and moral implications?

Also, our preservice teaching students demonstrated that when called upon to demonstrate reflective thinking, they could do it. Future research is needed to investigate whether continued use of coaching during their student teaching results in a permanent reflective stance that transfers to the participants' use of reflection during their inservice experiences.

APPLICATION OF SKILLS

QUESTION #2: DO PRESERVICE TEACHERS ENGAGED IN PRESERVICE COACHING USE AND DISCUSS THE SKILLS AND STRATEGIES TAUGHT IN THEIR EDUCATION METHODOLOGY COURSES?

As with the other questions, the data used to answer this question were the students' lesson plans, Skill Application Forms, PQP Forms, transcript of the students' debriefing conferences, and the reflective summaries of the teacher and coach for each coaching episode. Below is a list of skills/strategies that the preservice teachers chose to be coached on, and/or which they discussed in their debriefing sessions and reflective summaries.

SKILLS AND STRATEGIES FOCUSED ON DURING COACHING

Webbing/Brainstorming

Placement of Vocabulary Instruction in Relation to the Reading

Cooperative Learning Interaction

Class Participation/Active Learning

Verbal Positive Reinforcement

Think-Pair-Share

Motivation

Improving Comprehension—silent vs. oral reading

Levels of Questions/Questioning Strategies

Clarity of Directions

Transitions between Lesson Activities

Establishing Purposes-for-Reading/Reader-Response

Classroom Management

Techniques for Visual vs. Auditory Learners

On-task Behavior

All of these skills and strategies are a part of the Curriculum I course in which these students were enrolled. Thus, students appear to be recalling, applying, and reflecting upon ideas they had learned about on campus. Coaching appears to give these students an avenue for immediate use of the knowledge presented in their education classes.

The skill most frequently examined is the ability of the preservice teacher to act as a facilitator of "active learning." Typically, two-thirds of the students in a class chose this as the focus of one of their coached lessons. This is the theme of the College of Education at Towson State University and is stressed in each Education course. We are encouraged, therefore, that so many students attempt application of "active learning" during their initial teaching experiences.

Each set of coaching reports for a semester evidenced that only one-third of the students were developing and using Skill Application Forms for collecting and reporting objective data. We concluded that some of our students had not adequately mastered understanding of the relationship between a skill and outcomes resulting from use of a skill. More attention needs to be given during teacher training to help the teachers and coaches discuss in their planning sessions the student performance outcomes that would demonstrate the teachers' successful implementation of a skill or strategy. For example, for the scenarios reported in Chapter 3: What behaviors would be evidence that the students were "motivated" during Teresa's lesson? What would the first graders do or not do that would indicate that Sharon was clear in her directions? What exactly is "effective delivery," and what would be the performance outcomes if Kathy were achieving effective delivery? Although not all skills or strategies require a formal Skill Application Form, deliberate attention to performance outcomes might help both the teacher and coach better focus their observations and delve deeper into the lesson. This might be accomplished by asking preservice teachers to articulate and put in writing during the planning conference their own operational definitions of the skill focus and the teacher or student behaviors they would expect to see in the lesson that would demonstrate effective demonstration of the skill or use of the strategy.

BENEFITS OF PEER COACHING

QUESTION #3: WOULD PRESERVICE TEACHERS, LIKE INSERVICE TEACHERS, SEE THE VALUE IN PEER COACHING? WHAT BENEFITS, IF ANY, WOULD THEY PERCEIVE?

In order to answer this question, we administered an open-ended questionnaire at the end of each semester asking the preservice teachers this question:

> *On a scale of 1 (I disliked the coaching experience), 2 (I did not care for it particularly), 3 (It was okay), 4 (I liked it very much), or 5 (I "loved" it), what was your overall reaction to the coaching process? Please explain your rating.*

Through frequency tabulations of the ratings, and pattern induction applied to the comments by us and a group of teacher/researchers who audited our results, we found that after the first semester (during which we refined our coaching model), an average of 93% of the students reported either 5 ("loved" it) or 4 (liked it very much). The remaining small percentage (approximately 7%) fell into the #3 rating (It was okay).

Explanatory comments revealed that students perceived the following as benefits of peer coaching:

1. *Providing feedback in applying new teaching skills*

Preservice teachers reported learning from the feedback of their coaches:

> *The class was math and the students were labeled as 'low.' They were also very active! For weeks I tried to adapt my lessons to find ways to use cooperative learning to help the students and to make practical use of limited time. Peer coaching gave me that extra pair of eyes to help me see the strengths of the lesson and to finally decide how I could improve.*

> *There's always a better way. When you have a peer observing something specific, you really get feedback on that skill.*

Preservice teachers also reported learning about teaching while serving as the coach:

It was great observing another student teacher. I learned a great deal while being the coach. For example, my partner used "thumbs up" for a correct answer and "thumbs down" for an incorrect one. This is a great idea for involving first graders. Also, observing her gave me insight into behavior problems. For example, when the students were talking and should not have been, she said, "I like the way Joey is working so quietly." I was able to observe the students' positive reactions to these approaches. I can now incorporate these ideas that I learned by watching her during coaching into my own teaching—which will help make my teaching better.

My partner is a well-prepared teacher. Her teaching style is a little more rigid than mine—a matter of personal preference. In fact, to the degree that she could stand to relax the atmosphere a little, I believe now, after coaching her, I could probably benefit from being a little more rigid!

My partner was very skillful when asking questions of higher order thinking and probing for more complete or correct answers. Since observing/coaching her, I have become more aware of my classroom questions and questioning techniques. I hope to improve in this area.

2. *Fostering a positive attitude toward collegiality*

I realized that I, as a teacher, have a responsibility to fellow teachers and the profession as a whole . . . I like being the coach and feeling like I can help another teacher to grow stronger.

Teachers need to share ideas—especially preservice teachers who are learning and attempting new teaching strategies. As a preservice teacher, I had one model—my cooperating teacher—until I participated in coaching. Then I had a chance to see how other strategies were applied in another room with another model.

Students also wrote testimonies of the collegial aspect of this project into their reflective summaries." For example, in the fourth scenario in Chapter 3, p. 57 Carmela wrote:

One of the most positive outcomes of this coaching session . . . was being able to share my doubts and feelings with someone else who was not only going through similar experiences, but had observed

*me and knew what I was talking about. It was so comforting to find
out that Kathy sometimes felt as if she had failed in teaching when
her lessons did not go exactly as she had planned them.*

3. *Enhancing students' self-confidence*

*My coach brought to my attention a lot of the good things I do while
teaching that I hadn't given myself credit for.*

*My coaching partner helped me especially when I was feeling very
low about a lesson.*

Carmela's coaching partner, Kathy, (Scenario #4, Chapter 3, p. 59) echoed the
sentiments students expressed in questionnaires when she wrote in her
"Reflective Decisions" statement:

*When I myself thought that my lesson went well, I was afraid it
might be just "in my head," but when Carmela said it was a good
lesson, I thought, "WOW!! Maybe it was good!"*

PROBLEMS WITH PEER COACHING

QUESTION #4: WHAT PROBLEMS WOULD PRESERVICE TEACH-ERS ENCOUNTER WITH THIS PEER COACHING PROCESS?

The questionnaire administered at the end of the semester also asked the
preservice teachers to respond to the question: "What problems did you
encounter in using peer coaching?" Many students reported no problems
with the peer coaching, but two patterns of difficulties from the preservice
teachers' perspective did surface.

1. *Fear of Offending Their Coaching Partner*

Peer coaches reported being sensitive to offending their teacher-partners
when they asked Clarifying Questions that expressed reservations about how
the student teacher had done something, and Leading Questions that
couched suggestions for improvement. The following response is typical of
students who had this concern:

*One has to be very careful how he/she states clarifying questions
and polishing statements. I did not want to insult the teacher with
my comments when I was coaching. . . I did not want to seem too
critical or too opinionated.*

We concluded, nevertheless, that the coaches were successful in not offending their partners. In response to this question about problems encountered, no teachers who engaged in the peer coaching reported being offended when their coaches offered non-directive, constructive criticism aimed at helping them apply skills or strategies. In fact, preservice teachers, in response to the rating of the coaching process, claimed that the suggestions were very beneficial.

It is our belief that the coaches' sensitivity is quite natural for novices who themselves are not feeling confident about their own teaching ability and for whom observing, analyzing, and critiquing the lessons of others is foreign to their behavior. Based on experience with inservice teachers in peer coaching teams, we observe that concern for the feelings of their partners helps to insure the continued use of the *non-directive* conferencing format (questions), as opposed to the coach lapsing into exposition (declarative statements). Declarations and criticisms would eliminate or reduce the reflective opportunities of the teacher and would transfer ownership of decisions from the teacher (where they belong) to the coach.

2. *Difficulty Thinking of Appropriate "Polish" Suggestions*

A second pattern of concern reported by students was their difficulty thinking of appropriate "polish" suggestions.

> *The only difficulty I had with coaching was thinking of suggestions for my partner. It was easy to praise but harder for me to suggest improvements.*

The irony of this concern is that in the questionnaires and the "Reflective Decisions" writings of the teachers, most students reported that the suggestions of their coaches had been helpful and many reported success when they implemented the suggestions. Daphne (Chapter I, p. 12), in her "Reflective Decisions" wrote:

> *The main problem that I found in trying to teach my lesson was keeping the students' attention focused on the story during the group reading. My coach suggested that instead of having the students read the story orally, I should have them read one paragraph at a time silently, and then ask specific questions after they read one page. I agreed and have since tried that method. It works very well*

in keeping the attention of the students, as well as in aiding their comprehension of the story.

Another student reported that after her first lesson, her coach helped her realize that her classroom discipline needed more deliberate attention. She wrote:

. . . after talking with and watching my coach, I have several ideas about controlling movement and my voice variations that I can try next week.

Her peer coaching report, after her second teaching episode began:

Today's lesson was much better! I couldn't have asked for better discipline today.

It was typical to read statements like the following:

First of all, I feel that peer coaching is a very beneficial tool that should be used by all individuals in the teaching profession. Not only did Jane act as a coach for me with the two lessons she observed, but she also has been a great support system throughout the entire semester. I was not offended by any of her remarks, because I knew there were areas in my lessons that needed improvement. She made suggestions that I may have never thought of!

It is neither atypical nor alarming for students in the early stages of their professional development to find it *difficult* to think of lesson improvements. In the college classroom, we draw this concern to the surface and assure our students that recalling appropriate polish suggestions may not always automatically occur to them, for their experience in using and observing teaching skills and strategies is limited. Further, they have not yet taken all of the methodology courses during which they will gain knowledge of, and experience with, additional skills and strategies. We try to impress on them that what is most essential in this process is developing a reflective disposition to their own lessons and those of the teachers they coach so that self-directed growth can occur.

As the preservice teachers complete each coaching segment and submit their materials to us, we select exemplary ones and occasionally share selections with the entire class. This serves as a model for students' future work, and it also reinforces their sense of competence.

As we find coaching materials that reveal inappropriate suggestions or transcripts that reveal a stumped coaching pair, we use the material to conference with the students privately, or anonymously (and with permission from the student-authors) in class to solve the problem. The following transcript segment is from the debriefing conference of a coach and a teacher. It is the type of transcript that reveals a plea for help on classroom management from the Professor in a conference or all-class discussion session:

TEACHER: I had to keep telling them to go back and sit down. I couldn't get them to stay in their seats.

COACH: I felt so sorry for you. I kept thinking, "How can I help?"

TEACHER: No matter what I tried, it wouldn't change.

COACH: You obviously tried different methods and you just have to settle for what you can manage the best.

TEACHER: I have absolutely no idea how I could redo it, unless I just tell them, "Look, stay in your seats. When I'm finished checking one, raise your hand and I'll come around." I figure after a while it would dawn on me who had their hands up the longest.

COACH: You're right. There must be a better way!!!

PREPARING SUPERVISING TEACHERS FOR PRESERVICE PEER COACHING

During the first year of our study, we also queried the students' supervising teachers through an open-ended questionnaire about their perceptions of preservice peer coaching. The primary benefit reported was how peer coaching fostered collegial spirit and enhanced self-confidence for the preservice teachers. For example, one supervising teacher wrote:

> . . . *the biggest benefit was for the preservice teachers to feel like they are not alone in having to solve problems; to know that others are experiencing hurdles also is so important.*

The supervising teachers' questionnaire also asked them to respond to this question: "From your perspective, what problems were associated with this coaching project?" One concern had to do with the preservice teachers' adequate background as is expressed in this typical response:

I'm not sure if the curriculum students are qualified to critique each other's lessons. Teaching is a complex task and in order to peer coach one another, the students must be more proficient.

The supervising teachers queried seemed to view the preservice teachers as blank slates when they arrived in their classrooms. They were apparently unaware of the extensive knowledge base in pedagogy students were receiving in their methodology courses and of the training in reflection these students had received. We knew their perceptions were not accurate. The preservice teachers' lesson plans, the transcripts of their debriefing conferences, the PQP forms and the reflective summaries show that these teacher education students can, indeed, "critique each other's lessons" and their own. In fact, considering that this field experience is early in the student's professional development sequence, we continue to be impressed with the nature and variety of the preservice peer coach's feedback and with the insights the preservice teachers articulate in their reflective statements.

We also inferred from reading the responses of the supervising teachers on the questionnaire that some resented being excluded from this coaching experience. It was as if they resented someone other than themselves assuming their role as coach of a preservice student.

We certainly believe that supervising teachers are in a better position than preservice education students to offer suggestions to polish the instructional delivery of preservice students. At the same time, peer collaboration accomplishes purposes that cannot be accomplished in a hierarchical relationship of age, status, and experience. Rather than an "either . . . or" situation, we recommend both coaching with a peer and coaching by the supervising teacher. In this way, the preservice teacher reaps the skill application and collegial benefits of working with a peer, as well as the pedagogical wisdom of a veteran professional. For example, a preservice teacher might first debrief the lesson with his/her preservice coach, then engage in a conference with the supervising teacher. The preservice teacher-coach might also attend this conference with the supervising teacher and benefit from the veteran's comments.

The harsh reality was that these questionnaires told us loudly and clearly that we had been appropriately concerned about preparing the preservice teachers for peer coaching, but that we had neglected to prepare their supervising teachers. This information alerted us to the importance of informing (and in some cases, educating) supervising teachers about coaching, in general, and about this peer coaching project, specifically.

Now we make every effort to contact supervising teachers (individually or in groups) and to introduce them to the preservice peer coaching component of the field experience. We have learned that explaining the following aspects of coaching to the supervising teachers results in better understanding and support of the process:

1. Overviewing the college course content so supervising teachers are aware of the knowledge preservice teachers bring to this field experience.

2. Reviewing the successful history of peer coaching with inservice teachers (as reported in Chapter I) to provide credibility to the peer coaching component of the field experience.

3. Explaining the preservice teachers' peer coaching assignment (lesson plan, planning conference, peer-coach observation, tape and transcript of the debriefing conference, and reflective statement for at least two lessons) so supervising teachers understand and support the scheduling needed to fulfill these requirements.

4. Explaining the three purposes of the peer coaching assignment (to foster reflection, apply skills, and facilitate collegiality and self-confidence), so supervising teachers better understand their role in relation to the role of the preservice teacher-coach.

5. Sharing one or two exemplary transcripts and/or reflective statements so supervising teachers have a realistic perception of the preservice teachers' reflective capabilities at this point in their professional development.

6. Encouraging supervising teachers to continue fostering reflection with their preservice teachers when they conference with them about a lesson by:

   • beginning the conference by asking the preservice teacher, "What do you think was effective in your lesson?" and "What changes would you make in your lesson?"

   • giving Praise Comments and asking Clarifying, Eliciting and Leading Questions.

HOW TEACHER EDUCATORS CAN USE THIS INFORMATION

During the peer-coaching process, we accomplished several goals. Student teachers moved from nonreflection to reflection about their teaching; they applied teaching skills in which they had been instructed in their college courses, but which they had had no opportunity to incorporate into their active teaching repertoires; they discovered the advantages of a collegial approach to teaching.

When you are ready to embark on this adventure, you will, no doubt, want to read for yourself some of the primary sources on active learning, reflection, and coaching that are discussed and referenced in this text. A bibliography is included below for that purpose. Next, refer to Chapter 4 for information about training students to participate in peer coaching. A re-reading of the material in Chapters 1, 2, and 3 will help you shape your knowledge base as the foundation for what you can design and build with your own students. You will then need to inform supervising teachers in the field setting about the preservice teachers' coaching experiences in their classrooms. The understanding, acceptance, and support of cooperating teachers are essential to the success of this assignment. Refer to Chapter 5 for aspects that you will want to include in your briefing of the supervising teachers.

After the coaching activities have been completed, you will want to analyze the student teachers' products of this effort: lesson plans, PQP forms, Skill Application Forms, tapes and transcripts of the debriefing conferences, reflective statements. Refer to Chapter 1 for information about the processes of reflection that you may note in their reports. The insights that you gain will be excellent springboards for one-on-one conferences between yourself and each preservice teacher in your class.

As a culmination to the peer-coaching adventure, be sure to make class time for round-table discussions among your students of their peer-coaching efforts. They enjoy hearing about one another's experiences in the classroom, and they continue to learn more about the intricacies of "the art of teaching."

NEW TEACHERS'
PEER COACHING WORKBOOK

WORKSHEET #1
KNOWLEDGE ABOUT COACHING

Read Chapters 1, 2, and 3 of this text. Your professor may also ask you to read two Phi Delta Kappa fastbacks: #277 *Improving Teching through Coaching* (1988) and #371 *Peer Coaching in Teacher Education* (1994). Answer the following reader-response questions based on the knowledge you acquire from these readings. Be prepared to discuss these questions in class:

1. In your own words, explain "peer coaching."

2. What are the benefits of peer coaching? What benefit is most important to you?

3. Select one peer coaching scenario reported in the readings that impressed you the most. Why did it impress you?

4. What questions tdo you have about peer coaching?

WORKSHEET #2
SKILL FOCUS LIST

1. Based on lesson plans you have written for this and previous courses, and on micro-teaching and field-based teaching experiences, make a list of your perceived teaching strengths.

2. What teaching strategies, skills, or approaches have you studied, and have found interesting or challenging, but have not yet attempted or mastered?

3. Review your responses to #1 and #2 above. Now make a list of three to five teaching skills, strategies, or approaches that you would like to be coached on during this peer coaching project.

1.

2.

3.

4.

5.

Worksheet #3
COACHING COMMENTS

Part A: Classify each of the following coaching comments as one of the following: *Praise, Clarifying Question, Eliciting Question, Leading Question.*

1. What other forms of grouping could you have used to encourage more participation from the less able students?

    _____

2. The math problems that the students were to solve worked well because they were sequenced from the easy to the more difficult.

    _____

3. What do you think would happen if you had given students nonexamples as well as examples of polygons?

    _____

4. Why did you choose to use a web for this writing assignment?

    _____

5. Using the two composition models—one with specific detain and one wtihout specific detail—was excellent. I'm sure the students will emember what they learned about the effectiveness of detail because they were so involved in contrasting the two models.

    _____

6. Why did you choose not to give the students copies of the song lyrics, as you had originally planned?

    _____

7. Do you think Robert would have been more cooperative if he had been part of the second group?

    _____

Part B: Rewrite the following coaching comments to make them more effective. Remember to make *Praise Comments* that tell what and why; formulate **all** *Questions* to put ownership of the decision into the hands of the teacher.

1. Using a semantic web was good for these students.

    _____

    _____

    _____

2. Why did you use this awful story?

    _____

    _____

    _____

3. If I were going to teach this lesson, I would have used a directed reading approach.

    _____

    _____

    _____

4. There was too much commotion during group work. Why don't you have the students work alone for the next several classes?

    _____

    _____

    _____

WORKSHEET #4
PRAISE–QUESTION–POLISH COACHING FORM

Teacher _____   Coach _____

Date _____   School _____

Class/Period _____

Skill Focus _____

- -

PRAISE   (What went well? why was it effective?)

QUESTION   (Clarifying Questions: What is not clear? Eliciting Questions: What needs to be explored for change or variety?)

POLISH   (Questions that imply suggestions)

BIBLIOGRAPHY

ACTIVE LEARNING

Barnes, Douglas. *From Communication to Curriculum*. New York: Penguin Books, 1984.

Bonwell, Charles C. and James A. Eison. *Active Learning: Creating Excitement in the Classroom*. ASHE-ERIC Higher Education Report No. 1. Washington, D.C.: The George Washington University, School of Education and Human Development, 1991.

Chickering, Arthur W., and Zelda F. Gamson. "Seven Principles for Good Practice," *AAHE Bulletin*, XXXIX (March, 1987): 3-7. [ED 282 491]

Harmin, Merrill. *Inspiring Active Learning: A Handbook for Teachers*. Alexandria, Virginia: Association for Supervision and Curriculum Development, 1994.

Kagan, Jerome. "Learning, Attention and the Issue of Discovery," in *Learning by Discovery: A Critical Appraisal*, edited by Lee S. Shulman and Evan R. Keislar. Chicago: Rand McNally, 1966.

Neilsen, Allan R. *Critical Thinking and Reading: Empowering Learners to Think and Act*. Monograph on Teaching Critical Thinking, no. 2. Bloomington, Indiana: ERIC Clearinghouse on Reading and Communication Skills, and Urbana, Illinois: National Council of Teachers of English, 1989.

Neubert, Gloria A. and James B. Binko. *Encouraging Inductive Reasoning in the Secondary Classroom*. Washington, D.C.: National Education Association, 1992.

Resnick, Lauren B. *Education and Learning to Think*. Washington, D.C.: National Academy Press, 1987.

Smith, Frank. "The Politics of Ignorance," in *Essays Into Literacy*, edited by Frank Smith. Portsmouth, New Hampshire: Heinemann, 1983.

_____. *Insult to Intelligence*. Portsmouth, New Hampshire: Heinemann, 1986.

Stover, Lois T., Gloria A. Neubert and James C. Lawlor. *Creating Interactive Environments in the Secondary School*. Washington, D.C.: National Education Association, 1993.

COACHING

Baker, Robert G. and Beverly Showers. "The Effects of a Coaching Strategy on Teachers' Transfer of Training to Classroom Practice: A Six-Month Follow-up." Paper presented at the American Educational Research Association, New Orleans, April 1984.

Brandt, Ronald S. (ed.). *Coaching and Staff Development: Readings from Educational Leadership*. Alexandria, Virginia: Association for Supervision and Curriculum Development, 1989.

Joyce, Bruce and Beverly Showers. "Improving Inservice Training: The Messages of Research," *Educational Leadership*, XXXVII, 5 (February, 1980): 379-385.

Lyons, Bill. "The PQP Method of Responding to Writing," *English Journal*, LXX, 3 (March, 1981): 42-3.

McAllister, Elizabeth. "Metacognitive Planners in the 1990's," *MATE Journal*, IV (Spring 1990): 25-7.

Neubert, Gloria A. *Improving Teaching through Coaching*. Fastback #277. Bloomington, Indiana: Phi Delta Kappa Educational Foundation, 1988.

_____ and Elizabeth McAllister. "Peer Coaching in Preservice Education," *Teacher Education Quarterly*, XX, 4 (Fall, 1993): 77-84.

_____ and Sally J. McNelis. "Improving Writing in the Disciplines," *Educational Leadership*, XLIII, 7 (April, 1986): 54-58.

_____ and Lois T. Stover. *Peer Coaching in Teacher Education.* Fastback #371. Bloomington, Indiana: Phi Delta Kappa Educational Foundation, 1994.

Pavelich, Barbara. "Peer Coaching within the Internship." Monograph 10. Saskatchewan, Canada: Saskatchewan University, College of Education, 1992. [ED 354 216]

Robbins, Pam. *How to Implement a Peer Coaching Program.* Alexandria, Virginia: Association for Supervision and Curriculum Development, 1991.

Strother, Deborah Burnett (ed.). *Teacher Peer Coaching.* Center on Evaluation, Development, and Research. Hot Topic Series. Bloomington, Indiana: Phi Delta Kappa, 1989.

Wynn, Margie. "Peer Coaching in Early Field Experience," Paper presented at the Annual Meeting of the Eastern Educational Research Association, Sarasota, Florida, 1994.

REFLECTION

Beyer, Landon E. "Field Experience, Ideology, and the Development of Critical Reflectivity," *Journal of Teacher Education*, XXXV, 3 (May-June, 1984): 36-41.

Bullough, Robert V. Jr. "Teacher Education and Teacher Reflectivity," *Journal of Teacher Education*, XL, 2 (March-April, 1989): 15-21.

Canning, Christine. "What Teachers Say about Reflection," *Educational Leadership*, XLVIII, 6 (March, 1991): 18-21.

Cruickshank, Donald R., et al. *Reflective Teaching.* Bloomington, Indiana: Phi Delta Kappa, 1981.

Dewey, John. *The Relation of Theory to Practice in Education.* (Third Yearbook of NSSE). Bloomington, Indiana: Public School Publishing Co., 1904.

_____. *How We Think.* Chicago: Henry Regnery Co., 1933.

Ferguson, Patrick. "A Reflective Approach to the Methods Practicum," *Journal of Teacher Education*, XL, 2 (March-April, 1989): 36-41.

Giroux, H. "Teacher Education and the Ideology of Social Control," *Journal of Education*, 162: 5-27.

Goodman, Jesse. "Reflection and Teacher Education: A Case Study and Theoretical Analysis," *Interchange*, XV, 3, 1984: 9-26.

Gore, Jennifer M. "Reflecting on Reflective Teaching," *Journal of Teacher Education*, (March-April, 1987): 33-39.

Heesen, Berrie. "Critical Thinking and Humor," *Inquiry*, Newsletter of the Institute for Critical Thinking, Montclair State College, V, 1 (February, 1990): 3.

Liston, Daniel P. and Kenneth M. Zeichner. "Reflective Teacher Education and Moral Deliberation," *Journal of Teacher Education*, XXXVIII, 6 (November-December, 1987): 2-8.

McCarthy, Lucille Parkinson and Stephan M. Fishman. "Boundary Conversations: Conflicting Ways of Knowing in Philosophy and Interdisciplinary Research," *Research in the Teaching of English*, XXV, 4 (December, 1991): 419-468.

Neubert, Gloria A. and James B. Binko. "Teach-Probe-Revise: A Model for Initiating Classroom Research," *The Teacher Educator*, XXII, 1 (Summer, 1986): 9-17.

Pasch, M. T., et al., "Evaluating Teachers' Instructional Decision Making." Paper presented at the annual meeting of the Michigan Educational Research Association, Novi, Michigan, 1990.

Ross, Dorene Doerre. "First Steps in Developing A Reflective Approach," *Journal of Teacher Education*, XL, 2 (March- April, 1989): 22-30.

Roth, Rita and Susan Adler. "Critical Inquiry in Teacher Preparation," Paper presented at the Annual Meeting of the American Educational Research Association, Chicago, Illinois, 1985. [ED 264 187]

Roth, Robert A. "Preparing the Reflective Practitioner: Transforming the Apprentice through the Dialectic," *Journal of Teacher Education*, XXXX, 2 (March-April, 1989): 31-35.

Rudney, Gwen L. and Andrea M. Guillaume. "Reflective Teaching for Student Teachers," *The Teacher Educator*, XXV, 3 (Winter, 1989-90): 13-20.

Schon, Donald. *Educating the Reflective Practitioner*. San Francisco: Jossey-Bass Publishers, 1990.

Sparks-Langer, Georgea Mohlman and Amy Berstein Colton. "Synthesis of Research on Teachers' Reflective Thinking," *Educational Leadership*, XLVIII, 6 (March, 1991): 37-44.

Tom, A. R. *Teaching as a Moral Craft*. New York: Longman, 1984.

Van Manen, M. "Linking Ways of Knowing with Ways of Being Practical," *Curriculum Inquiry*. VI, 6 (1977): 205-228.

Wildman, Terry M. and Jerome A. Niles. "Reflective Teachers: Tensions between Abstractions and Realities," *Journal of Teacher Education*, (July-August, 1987): 25-31.

Zeichner, Kenneth M. "Reflective Teaching and Field-Based Experiences in Teacher Education," *Interchange*, XII, 4 (1981-82): 1-22.

_____"Alternative Paradigms of Teacher Education," *Journal of Teacher Education*, XXXIV, 3 (May-June, 1983): 3-9.

_____and Daniel P. Liston. "Teaching Student Teachers to Reflect," *Harvard Educational Review*, LVII, 1 (February, 1987): 23-48.

_____and K. Teitelbaum. "Personalized and Inquiry-Oriented Teacher Education," *Journal of Education for Teaching*, VIII, 2 (1982), 95-117.

Elizabeth A. McAllister is Associate Professor of Elementary Education at Towson State University in Maryland, having taught at the elementary and college levels in Florida, Tennessee, and Maryland for 19 years. She completed her Ed. D. in Curriculum and Instruction/Reading/Language Arts at the University of Florida in Gainesvile. In addition to numerous articles and conference presentations, Dr. McAllister's publications include *Primary Skills Activities Kit* (Prentice-Hall, 1987), *Peer Teaching and Collaborative Learning in the Language Arts* (ERIC/RCS, 1990), and *Learning Together: Collaboration for Active Learning in the Elementary Language Arts* (ERIC/REC, 1995). Her research interests extend to cognitive and metacognitive learning, auditory and visual perception, metalinguistics and language development, reading and language-arts strategies, peer teaching in the classroom and peer coaching for teachers preparing to teach.

Gloria A. Neubert is Professor of Education at Towson State University in Maryland. She received a B.S. in English and an M.Ed. in Secondary Education from Towson State University, and after teaching at the secondary level, she earned the Ph.D. in Reading with a concentration in Staff Development from the University of Maryland. Dr. Neubert's professional interests include preservice and inservice training effectiveness and reading and writing instruction. She is the author of PDK Fastback 277 (1988): *Improving Teaching through Coaching* and numerous articles, and coauthor (with J. B. Binko) of *Inductive Reasoning in the Secondary School* (NEA, 1992)

The TRIED™ series from ERIC/EDINFO Press puts fresh and effective lesson ideas into your hands!

Each TRIED is a collection of alternatives to textbook teaching designed and tested by your teaching peers. Assembled from entries in the ERIC database—the largest educational retrieval system in existence—TRIEDs make it easy to tap into the professional expertise and experience of the nation's finest educators.

Teaching Literature by Women Authors

Expands literature-based learning to include important works of 29 women. Strategies develop a sense of gender equity and teach the novels, stories, and poems of Madeline L'Engle, Toni Morrison, Anne Frank, and other women of the past and present. (Elem./Mid./Sec.)

AT14; 224 pp.; $16.95

Teaching Values through Teaching Literature

Presents teaching strategies for today's most powerful instructional materials, including novels, folk literature, poetry, and ethnic literature. Features a section on setting up a program in values clarification through literature. (Mid./Sec.)

AT13; 168 pp.; $16.95

Reading and Writing across the High School Science and Math Curriculum

Exciting reading and writing alternatives to the textbook approach. Explore lessons on "writing to learn" in math and science: journal writing, scientific poetry writing, and using writing to overcome those dreaded "story problems." (Sec.)

AT12; 132 pp.; $16.95

Celebrate Literacy! The Joy of Reading and Writing

Covers the full range of language-arts strategies and literature to turn your elementary school into a reading-and-writing carnival including literacy slumber parties, book birthdays, and battles of the books. (Elem.)

AT11; 92 pp.; $14.95

Working with Special Students in English/Language Arts

Helps take the worry out of teaching special students. Strategies to organize your classroom; use computers; implement cooperative learning; and teach thinking skills, reading, and writing to students with special needs. (Elem./Mid./Sec.)

AT10; 71 pp.; $14.95

A High School Student's Bill of Rights

Invites middle and high school students to explore the U.S. Constitution and other bodies of law. Lesson approaches are focused on precedent-setting legal cases that have dealt with students' rights when they were contested in the school context. May be used as a whole course, a mini-course, or as supplementary activities. (Mid./Sec.)

AT09; 117 pp.; $14.95

Reading Strategies for the Primary Grades

Presents a storehouse of clever ideas to begin reading and writing, and to build vocabulary and comprehension. Uses stories, poems, response logs, oral reading, Whole Language, and much more! (Elem.)

AT08; 102 pp.; $14.95

Language Arts for Gifted Middle School Students

Supplies challenging lessons in a variety of language arts areas: communication skills, literature, mass media, theater arts, reading, writing. Activities designed for gifted students also work for others. (Mid.)

AT07; 74 pp.; $14.95

Remedial Reading for Elementary School Students

Uses games and reading activities to stimulate imagination, develop reading skills, and strengthen comprehension. (Elem.)

AT05; 76 pp.; $14.95

Writing Exercises for High School Students

Motivates students to explore creative, descriptive, and expository writing. Introduces the young writer to all the basics of good writing. (Sec.)

AT04; 81 pp.; $14.95

Critical Thinking, Reading, and Writing

Encourages reading, writing, and thinking in a critically reflective, inventive way for students at all levels. Practical classroom activities make critical thinking an achievable goal. (Elem./Mid./Sec.)

AT03; 96 pp.; $14.95

Teaching the Novel

Offers strategies for teaching many novels, including To Kill a Mockingbird, The Color Purple, The Scarlet Letter, *and other oft-taught works of interest to middle school and high school students. (Mid./Sec.)*

AT02; 88 pp.; $14.95

Writing across the Social Studies Curriculum

Strategies to connect writing activities with lessons on important topics in the social studies. Includes U.S. History, World History, Newspapers, Geography, etc. (Mid./Sec.)

AT01; 101 pp.; $14.95

Writing Is Learning

Strategies for Math, Science, Social Studies, and Language Arts

by Howard Wills

Today's teachers know that writing isn't just a subject to be taught. Writing is an effective tool for teaching in any content area—and a powerful way to make students active participants in their own learning.

Hear from both students and teachers about how they enjoy and benefit from using writing to learn math, science, social studies, and language arts.

Discover specific strategies for

- saving teacher evaluation and teaching time
- reinforcing learning
- peer review and response
- relating prior knowledge to new information
- finding real-world applications
- encouraging analytical and critical thinking

Writing activities include

- journals
- writing "from the future"
- narratives
- reviews

- problem solving
- summaries
- definitions
- letter writing

"This book will serve well all subject teachers who want ideas and examples for using writing in their classrooms, and it will give administrators glimpses of classrooms where students are indeed actively involved in their own learning."

—Carl B. Smith
Director, ERIC/REC

Softcover, 6 x 9 in., 160 pp.
BWIL; $14.95

Quiet Children and the Classroom Teacher

(Second Edition)

by James McCroskey and Virginia Richmond

Analyzes why some children are quiet and teaches teachers how to overcome "communication apprehension" to insure that quiet children learn. Shows the teacher how to communicate with quiet students and how to draw them out without causing them to dive deeper into their shyness and quietness.

Copublished with the Speech Communication Association.

Softcover, 6 x 9 in., 60 pp.
AG27; $9.95

Teaching Kids to Care
Exploring Values through Literature and Inquiry
by Sharon Vincz Andrews

This hands-on guide for elementary and middle school teachers offers clear directions for exploring values using children's literature as a starting point. Two case studies—a sixth-grade class studying AIDS and a third-grade class studying homelessness—demonstrate that when students choose topics and directions for the discovery of values, their motivation for learning becomes real.

Combining classroom examples and practical advice, backed up by historical analysis and educational theory, *Teaching Kids to Care* includes

- **Discussion of crucial questions:** What is a value? Whose values should we teach? How should we teach them?
- **Clear examples** of how inquiry- and literature-based investigations of values work in classrooms
- **Instructional strategies** that promote self-directed discovery of values
- **A unique annotated bibliography** of literature that guides children in their values exploration
- **Analysis of textbooks** and their connection to moral education

Softcover, 8¹/₂ x 11 in., 256 pp.
AG55; $19.95

Peer Teaching and Collaborative Learning in the Language Arts
by Elizabeth McAllister

Six real-life scenarios illustrate how teachers have successfully implemented peer teaching and collaborative learning in the classroom. By sharing and cooperating, students gain more knowledge and sharpen their skills, and they learn from one another how to learn.

Describes four ways of organizing a peer-teaching program, offers suggestions on how to train tutors and design tutoring lessons, and explains how to evaluate the effects of a program in cooperative learning. Includes sample evaluation and accomplishment forms and a delightfully illustrated "Indiana Jones" map of peer-tutorial progress. (Elem./Mid.)

> *"Teachers will find many specific ideas in this book to use in their schools and classrooms and to adapt into their own programs. Elizabeth McAllister not only tells how to do things but also explains the principles behind the practices. This book should be a constant reference source in every teacher's professional library."*
>
> —Roger Farr
> Indiana University

Softcover, 8¹/₂ x 11 in., 65 pp.
AG13; $15.95

Becoming a Teacher
A Practical and Political School Survival Guide
by Robin Grusko and Judy Kramer

A guide for new teachers about to take the plunge into the real world of teaching. Grusko and Kramer identify safe passages around the potential pitfalls that await new teachers—decisions about what to do on the first day in a new teaching job, how to deal with administrators, knowing which coworkers to trust, joining teachers' unions, relations with parents, and more.

This illustrated book shows new teachers the ropes with wry humor, common sense, and candor that suits the stressful but rewarding experiences that beginning teachers face.

> *"No one told us this stuff! . . . I hope you get it out there quickly to help new soldiers in the trenches."*
>
> —Russ Gurle
> *Teacher of the Year 1993*
> Pauls Valley High School, Oklahoma

> *"Very open and informative about the realities of teaching in a political system."*
>
> —Elizabeth McAllister
> Professor of Teacher Education
> Towson State University, Maryland

Softcover, 6 x 9 in., 138 pp.
AG46; $14.95

Writing for Successful Publication
by Kenneth T. Henson

An insider's grasp of how to get published in professional journals by a widely published expert who monitors and reports on publication in the field of education.

> *"A must book! Anyone in the educational community who would like to write or must write to maintain or upgrade their position would benefit from reading this book!"*
>
> —Jesus Garcia
> Associate Professor
> School of Education, Indiana University

Copublished with National Educational Service.

Softcover, 6 x 9 in., 263 pp.
AG23; $21.95

ORDER FORM

Qty.		Price	Subtotal

The TRIED™ Series:

____	Teaching Literature by Women Authors (AT14) $16.95	_____
____	Teaching Values through Teaching Literature (AT13) 16.95	_____
____	Reading and Writing across the High School Science and Math Curriculum (AT12) 16.95	_____
____	Celebrate Literacy! The Joy of Reading and Writing (AT11) 14.95	_____
____	Working with Special Students in English/Language Arts (AT10) . 14.95	_____
____	A High School Student's Bill of Rights (AT09) 14.95	_____
____	Reading Strategies for the Primary Grades (AT08) 14.95	_____
____	Language Arts for Gifted Middle School Students (AT07) 14.95	_____
____	Remedial Reading for Elementary School Students (AT06) 14.95	_____
____	Writing Exercises for High School Students (AT05) 14.95	_____
____	Critical Thinking, Reading, and Writing (AT03) 14.95	_____
____	Teaching the Novel (AT02) 14.95	_____
____	Writing across the Social Studies Curriculum (AT01) 14.95	_____

Other titles for teachers:

____	Writing Is Learning (BWIL) 14.95	_____
____	Quiet Children and the Classroom Teacher (AG27) 9.95	_____
____	Teaching Kids to Care (AG55) 19.95	_____
____	Peer Teaching and Collaborative Learning in the Language Arts (AG13) 15.95	_____
____	Becoming a Teacher (AG46) 14.95	_____
____	Writing for Successful Publication (AG23) 21.95	_____

Subtotal	_____
Add 10% for S&H (minimum charge is $3.00)	_____
Indiana residents add 5% sales tax	_____
ORDER TOTAL	_____

Order by mail, phone, or FAX!
Please turn the page and complete ordering information.

To place your order, please mail, phone, or FAX to:

Mail: **ERIC/EDINFO Press**
Indiana University
P.O. Box 5953
Bloomington, IN 47407

Phone: **1-800-925-7853**
(M–F, 8:00 a.m. – 5:00 p.m. EST)

FAX: **1-812-331-2776**

Ship to:

Name	
Title	
Organization	
Address	
City/State/ZIP	
Phone	

Method of Payment

❑ check   ❑ money order   ❑ **VISA**   ❑ **MasterCard**   ❑ **DISCOVER**

❑ P.O.# _____

Cardholder	
Card Number	Exp. Date
Cardholder's Signature	

YOUR SATISFACTION IS GUARANTEED

If for any reason you are not completely satisfied with a product or
publication you purchase from us, simply return the item within 30 days
and we will refund your money.